MARY DYER
Biography of
a Rebel Quaker

by
Ruth Talbot Plimpton

BRANDEN BOOKS, Boston

Library of Congress Cataloging-in-Publication Data

Plimpton, Ruth Talbot, 1916-
    Mary Dyer : biography of a rebel Quaker /
       by Ruth Talbot Plimpton.
        p. cm.
    Includes bibliographical references (p. xxx-xxx)
       and index.
    ISBN 0-8283-1964-2 : $21.95 (Hardback)
    ISBN 9780828322089: $19.95 (Paperback)
    1. Dyer, Mary, d. 1660.
    2. Quakers--Massachusetts--Boston--Biography.
    3. Christian martyrs--Massachusetts--Boston
       --Biography.
    4. Freedom of religion--Massachusetts--History--
       17th century.
    5. Boston (Mass.)--Biography. I. Title.
BX7795.D84P57 1994
272'.8'092--dc20   93-38000
[B]   CIP

BRANDEN BOOKS P O Box 812094 Wellesley MA 02482
www.brandenbooks.com

Contents

Illustrations

Acknowledgments

My thanks go to Peggy Brooks for editorial help over several years. I am also grateful to Aileen Ward, as leader of a writers' workshop. I treasure the stimulating exchange between my fellow writers, with special appreciation to Natalie Dymnicki, Paige Kempner, and Sally Wriggins.

My research led me through the stacks of many a library where I was helped by lots of librarians. I would like to give special thanks to those who work in my three favorite haunts: the Society Library in New York City, the Redwood Library in Newport, Rhode Island, and the New England Historic Genealogical Society in Boston, Massachusetts.

There have been many very helpful readers and critics of my manuscript. One person has had constant input with her legal accuracy, artistic style and tremendous caring. Thank you, Polly.

for Cal

INTRODUCTION

We think of America as a country born in the Pilgrims' search for religious freedom and committed ever since to toleration of differing beliefs. The story of Mary Dyer, as so movingly told by Ruth Plimpton, shows how idealized--how false--that historical image is. Mary Dyer was hanged in Boston because of her Quaker beliefs. And it was a rather democratic government, chosen by the male citizens of the Massachusetts Bay colony, that ordered her execution.

From the beginning there has been a dark streak in American democracy: a popular intolerance of nonconforming ideas. Puritans dominated the group of Pilgrims who landed at Plymouth in 1620, and Puritans formed the Massachusetts Bay Company that ruled the colony from 1630 to 1684. They were dissenters from the established Church of England, wishing to purify the church of what they deemed corrupt practices. They left England to escape persecution--which is why we think of them as apostles of freedom. But they were utterly intolerant of religious views other than their own, which they enforced as the official faith of their colony.

The cruelty of the Puritan leaders of Massachusetts in their zeal to punish Quakers will no doubt shock contemporary readers. When their hanging of Mary Dyer was brought to the attention of King Charles the Second and he ordered them to "forebear to proceed any further" with the planned execution and imprisonment of other Quakers, they enforced an ingeniously cruel law that punished Quakers without naming them. The so-called Cart and Tail Law, it provided that any man or woman of a certain description found in Boston (in fact, Quakers) was to be stripped to the waist, fastened to the tail of a horse cart and whipped as he or she was dragged behind the cart up to the border of the colony.

But we must not fall into the fallacy of assuming that persecution of religious dissenters was unusual in the Seventeenth Century. To the contrary, it was the rule everywhere in the Christian world--and had been since the Emperor Valerian issued his decree of intolerance in the year 380, calling on all to believe in the holy Trinity and branding "all the senseless followers of other religions by the infamous name of heretics." The colony of Rhode Island was founded by men and women who wanted to escape from the theocratic tyranny of Massachusetts. In 1663, Rhode Islanders persuaded King Charles to give them a new charter providing that no person in that colony "shall be in any wise molested, punished, disquieted or called in Question for any Difference in Opinion in Matters of Religion." Mrs. Plimpton observes: "This was the first document in America, and possibly in Europe, to legalize freedom of religion."

Nor did American intolerance of differing beliefs end in the Seventeenth Century. A recurring feature of our history has been demagogic politicians playing on popular fear of "alien" ideas, religious or political. At the end of the Eighteenth Century, the bogeyman was French revolutionary Jacobism; Thomas Jefferson, when he ran for President in 1800, was accused of being not only a French sympathizer but an atheist. In the middle of the Nineteenth century, there were the Know Nothings, a nativist movement driven by fear of the Roman Catholic immigrants. Through much of the Twentieth Century, the devil was communism. Politicians from Attorney General A. Mitchell Palmer in 1920 to Senator Joseph R. McCarthy in the 1950's and 1960's fulminated against "godless communism." That opportunity for demagoguery did not end until the collapse of the Soviet Union. "The paranoid style in American politics," political scientist Richard Hofstadter called it.

In matters of religion, most of us believed that by the middle of this century America was safe for diversity. But since then there has come the rise of fundamentalism--Islamic, Jewish and Christian. Fundamentalists, like the Puritans of early Massachusetts, are certain that they have the only true faith. At the end of the century Christian fundamentalists, acting through increasingly powerful political groups, are trying to impose their certainties on the country.

So the struggle for which Mary Dyer gave her life, the struggle for every individual's freedom of belief, is not over. And it never will be. The greatest libertarian thinker in our history, Jefferson, thought the most important liberty for which he fought in a long lifetime was freedom of religious belief. One of his biographers, Henry Wilder Foote, called his campaign to that end "the severest struggle of Jefferson's career."

In 1776, at the time of the American Revolution, Virginia law still criminalized heresy; the Episcopal Church was the established religion, its ministers paid by the state. In that year, at the Virginia Convention, Jefferson proposed a draft constitution calling for "full and free liberty of religious opinion." The draft was not used, but the Convention did adopt a Bill of Rights one clause of which said that men are "entitled to the full and free exercise of religion, according to the dictates of conscience." Later that year the Legislature stopped paying Episcopal ministerial salaries. In 1777, Jefferson drafted a Statute for Religious Freedom. He introduced it as legislation in 1779 and subsequent years, but it ran into heavy resistance.

In his Notes on Virginia, Jefferson wrote: "Subject opinion to coercion, whom will you make your inquisitors' Fallible men, governed by bad passions, by private as well as public reasons. But is uniformity of opinion desirable' No more than of face or stature.... Difference of opinion is advantageous to religion.... The effect of coercion has been to make one half the world fools, and the other half hypocrites.... Reason and persuasion are the only practicable instruments by which men can be gathered into the fold of truth."

James Madison finally pushed the Statute for Religious Freedom through the Virginia legislature in 1786, when Jefferson was in France. It provides: "That no man shall be compelled to frequent or support any religious worship, place or ministry whatsoever, nor shall be enforced, restrained, molested, or burthened in his mind or goods, nor shall otherwise suffer on account of his religious opinions or beliefs; but that all men shall be free to possess, and by argument to maintain, their opinions in matters of religion, and that the same shall in nowise diminish, enlarge, or affect their civil capacities."

Jefferson designed his own burial monument, an obelisk that visitors can see at Monticello, his home near Charlottesville. He chose the inscription, listing achievements that he thought more important than being President of the United States: "Here was buried Thomas Jefferson, Author of the Declaration of American Independence, of the Statute of Virginia for religious freedom, & Father of the University of Virginia."

The life of Mary Dyer showed that freedom of conscience was as important to women as to men--and that a woman could be as courageous in the struggle for that freedom. She died for her beliefs, but in her death was victory. Her statue in front of the State House on Beacon Hill in Boston is as much a testament to freedom as the monument at Monticello.

ANTHONY LEWIS

{ 1 }
Questions of Heredity

"Let men of God, in Court and Church watch O'er such as do in toleration hatch."

This memo, found in the pocket of Thomas Dudley at his death in 1653, expressed the overriding anxiety of the Puritan leaders in Boston over the slightest suggestion of religious toleration. They left England with their own unshakable beliefs and, once in New England, created laws to get rid of anyone who did not conform with their religious interpretations. The punishment for breaking those laws increased from whipping, banishing, to killing.

Mary Dyer was hanged on Boston Commons in 1660 for being a Quaker. Writing in 1696, the Dutch historian, George DeCroese, described Mary Dyer as "a person of no mean extract or parentage, of an estate pretty plentiful, of a comely stature and countenance, of a piercing knowledge of many things, of a wonderful sweet and pleasant discourse, so fit for great affairs, that she wanted nothing that was manly, except only name and sex."[1]

It was an unusual description of a lady of the 17th century — or any other century. The tantalizing question is, who was she? Historical documents record the death of Mary Dyer in great detail, but precise information concerning her birth is mysteriously lacking.

Frederick Nathaniel Dyer, a lineal descendant of Mary, whose father was born in Rhode Island, was a respected historical researcher. He moved to Macclesfield, England, where he had many opportunities to investigate the family history.[2]

Be it legend or history, F.N. Dyer's story of Mary Dyer suggests reasons why this unusual woman came to lead such an extraordinary life.

When Queen Elizabeth died in 1603, she left no heirs. Succession shifted to other descendants of Henry VII, with James I, who was the son of Mary, Queen of Scots and Henry Stuart (Lord Darnley) succeeding. King James felt threatened by the equal eligibility of his first cousin, Arabella Stuart, daughter of Charles Stuart and Elizabeth Cavendish. Arabella had no desire to be Queen of England; she only wanted a loving husband, children, and a garden of her own. However, many suitors from England and France hoped that, by marrying her, they would capture the throne; some even hoped to restore Catholicism to England. These aggressive courtiers made King James so angry and anxious he prohibited his cousin, Arabella, from marrying anyone. But she fell in love with Sir William Seymour, also a descendant of Henry VII through the House of Suffolk, and third cousin to Arabella. They were secretly wed in 1610. Within a year, they had a daughter and the secret was out. King James became very disturbed that this marriage doubled Arabella's qualifications for the throne. In his fear, he ordered Arabella to be sent to Highgate, and William Seymour imprisoned in the Tower of London.

Arabella tried to run away from Highgate dressed as a man, but though she escaped from prison and boarded a ship to Calais, she was soon recaptured and sent to the Tower of London. There she spent the four remaining years of her life, without hope of reprieve. She was buried in Westminster Abbey in the Tomb of Mary, Queen of Scots, with whom she had lived after the early death of her parents.

William Seymour, Marquis of Hertford, escaped to France, and when he eventually returned to England, after the death of King James, his former history was forgotten, and he became tutor to the eleven-year-old Prince of Wales, the future King Charles II.

The infant girl was left in the care of Arabella's loving lady-in-waiting, Mistress Mary Dyer, who gave her own name to her adopted child and brought her up quietly and reclusively in the country. King James sent out scouts searching for the child, but was denied information by anyone who was questioned. When Mary was twenty-two years old, she married her foster mother's first cousin, William Dyer, descendant of Sir Richard Dyer, Lord of the manor of Wincarton, Somersetshire. This is the story that was told by Frederick Nathaniel Dyer and revealed in the Colonial Dames account, as well as the New England Historical and Genealogical Register 98 and the biography of Arabella Stuart, by Blanche Christabel Hardy.

Early Boston accounts report that Mary Dyer, who came to New England in 1635, was married to her cousin William Dyer. The names do not exactly correspond with the registry of St. Martins-in-the-Field in London, where the marriage of Marie Barrett and Guillaume Dyer was recorded and later the birth, baptism, and death of their son, William. Mary never called herself "Marie" in America, but one grandson was named "Barrett." William signed his name as "Guliel" (the French version of William) on one of the Rhode Island documents. Although the 17th Century spelling of names was prone to variety, it is curious that a couple like Mary and William would differ in the spelling of their last name; Mary used "Dyar" and William used "Dyre". The contradictions in reporting as well as the differentiation in spelling, make one wonder whether Mary was trying to conceal something of her heritage. Certainly it is not too great a stretch of the imagination to assume the historical Mary Dyer, who died in Boston, was the daughter of Arabella Stuart and William Seymour.

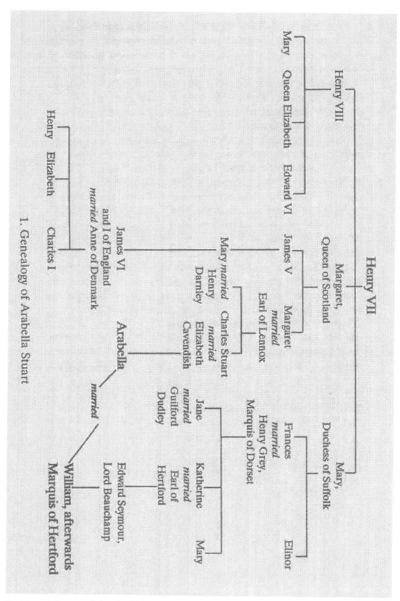

1. Genealogy of Arabella Stuart

{ 2 }
The Dyers
from Old to New England

This narrative centers on Mary Dyer's search for freedom of religion. The events, which were set in motion by King Henry VIII's split with the Roman Catholic Church in 1531, take place in England, Massachusetts Bay Colony, and Rhode Island between the years of 1635 and 1663. The King had assumed for himself and his heirs the right to rule the church as well as the state. In protest, many new religious sects evolved, seeking ways to reform the Anglican service and return to the simplicity of the early church, as a more genuine method of communicating with God. Those who worked to purify the church were known as Puritans. Believing that the Bible contained the whole word of God, it was their desire to purge the Anglican Church of the procession of bishops and any ceremonies for which there was no reference in the Bible. During the reign of Queen Elizabeth, the First English Prayer Book was designated as the only legal rule of worship for the Church of England. The non-conforming Puritans believed that this book, the Book of Common Prayer, altered the word of God and should be discarded; God's word could only be revealed by His Command, as written in the Bible.

In the 17th century, Puritan-minded ministers of the Church of England were dismissed for preaching new solutions for the church. Some dissenters were whipped, imprisoned, and even executed. Lacking any public place for discussion, the reformist Puritans retreated to secret hiding places to exchange ideas, deciding, finally, that there could be no satisfactory reform within the Church of

England. Another land was needed.

Several years before Mary Dyer was born, one protesting group had already split with the Mother Church and gone to Holland. Known as Separatists, they remained there for twelve years and then, when Mary was nine years old, these Pilgrims sailed across three thousand miles of ocean and settled in a place they called Plymouth.

When Mary was fourteen, in 1625, Charles I succeeded James I as King of England. We know that Mary had occasion to visit the royal court of King Charles I. The ball-gown that she made to wear for functions at Buckminster Palace is described as "a dress worked in many colored silks, with gold and silver thread, the groundwork of this dress was rich white satin [embroidered with] butterflies, flowers, grasshoppers [and] other insects.[1]" This gown must have been of great importance to Mary, for she tucked it among the articles she took with her upon her migration to New England in a small crowded ship. Pieces of this gown are reportedly still in the possession of some of Mary's descendants, as is a gold bodkin, engraved with the initials "M.D."[2]. The bodkin is a long needle with a wide slit and a blunt end which would have been used to make holes in cloth through which to thread ribbon or cord.

Mary belonged to the St. Martins-in-the-Field church, which registered the marriage of Marie Barrett and Guillaume Dyer on October 27, 1633, the baptism of their son, William, on October 24, 1634 and the burial of the infant on October 27, 1634.[3]

St. Martins-in-the-Field, with its stained glass windows, ornate altar, candles and organ music, was a significant part of Mary's religious heritage. However, the Dyers began to chafe under its administration. The appointed clergy were slavishly following the dictates of King Charles I, Archbishop Laud, and a whole line of conforming bishops, while the ministers of independent mind, who inspired the Dyers, were being silenced and suspended, one after another. Mary and William were not willing to submit to what they opposed. Yet there were no easy solutions for change in England.

Also contributing to the Dyer's need for change was William's work. He had just finished a nine-year apprenticeship in a branch of the Fishmonger's Guild, where he was apprenticed to a milliner,

William Blackburn.[4] In the 17th century, a "milliner" was someone who imported fineries from Milan. William had a business of selling small wares, such as pouches, broaches, daggers, swords, knives, French and Spanish gloves, spurs, capes and dials. When he finished his apprenticeship, times were bad in London, and William was looking for a change of occupation. As a member of the New Exchange in London, he was in touch with developments worldwide.

Through the New Exchange, William heard of a pastor in Dorchester, Wessex, called John White. White had organized a group of farmers and fishermen in a joint stock company, known as the Dorchester Adventurers, to sail to New England in 1626 and erect a fishing stage on Cape Anne, on the coast of Massachusetts. Fourteen men spent two cold, homesick, unhappy winters before they realized the combination of fishing and farming in one place by such a small group would not work. In 1628, the Dorchester Company dissolved, the majority returning to England. Roger Conant, who had been the manager of the plantation, stayed on and wrote John White that he saw possibilities for a Bible commonwealth for which he would like to explore new land. Moving to Naumkeag, Conant built some thatched cottages and garden lots to start a community.

Although the Dorchester Company had failed, John White remained interested in the idea of founding a colony in Massachusetts Bay. He persuaded 90 other men to join him in another venture, called the New England Company. After many trips to London, they received a patent granting them land purchased from Plymouth "lying between parallel lines three miles north of the Merrimac River and three miles south of the Charles River by the side of Massachusetts Bay." It was then proposed that one of their members, army-trained John Endicott, should create a fishing and trading plantation as a northern counterpart of the Virginia Colony. Landing in Naumkeag in 1628, hard-headed John Endicott took over Conant's position, as well as the homes he had built, and changed the Indian name of Naumkeag to the Hebrew name of Salem — meaning "peace."

Back in Dorchester, England, John White became concerned that the patent secured from Plymouth did not have the royal stamp to protect the latest enterprise from other would-be colonies looking for land along the New England coast. Succeeding the New England Company, the Massachusetts Bay Colony was formed to procure a Royal Charter which consolidated its position. The enterprising John Winthrop became interested in the colony that was being developed by John Endicott in Salem. Winthrop was a country squire from Groton, a staunch Puritan, who practiced law in London. When Charles I dissolved Parliament in 1629, John Winthrop lost his job with the Inner Temple. Having heard of John Endicott's success in starting a colony in Salem, and longing for a greater public service than the law offered, Winthrop decided to join the overseas experiment. He had his own priorities. In 1629, he gathered twelve men together to sign the Cambridge Agreement pledging that, if they could obtain the Royal Charter, they would emigrate with their families. March 16, 1629, King Charles I issued a charter incorporating the government and Company of Massachusetts Bay Colony in New England, a settlement of permanent dwellers in Massachusetts. The legal committee, the General Court and the Charter were all transferred to Massachusetts Bay. It was an ingenious stroke to give the Massachusetts Bay Colony civic independence while Winthrop and his followers slipped away from England with every promise to remain loyal to the Mother Church.

John Winthrop was made governor on October 20, 1629. In 1630 he, carrying his Royal Charter, set sail on the Arabella with 700 followers, known as the Massachusetts Bay Company.

John Winthrop's experiment in New England tempted the Dyers. Winthrop had a strong social conscience combined with his religious belief. He was not an impoverished man and his religion seemed to reach beyond the elegant processions of bishops to the multitude of deprived people everywhere, a philosophy which held great appeal for the Dyers. Moreover, he was not splitting with the English church like the Pilgrims of Plymouth, but his announced intentions were to return to the simpler Apostolic services and thereby set an example for all England to follow. Possibly, the way to reform St. Martins-in-the-Field would be to experiment with a different system in a distant location. Mary was thinking it over.

Letters received from the first settlers described New England as the most healthful place in the world, with extraordinary clean and dry air, springs of fresh water, magnificent woods along a shorefront complete with harbors, an abundance of islands, more fish than one could haul, fat juicy turkeys in the woods, and pumpkins, carrots, turnips, and parsnips larger and sweeter than those grown in England. Francis Higginson, minister of the First Congregational Church in Salem, wrote several such appealing letters back to England, describing only the "pleasures" of the New World — and promptly died of tuberculosis.

These letters arrived just after the death of the Dyer's firstborn son. By 1635, Mary was pregnant again and once more she and William were full of hope for a healthy child. New England sounded like a much more desirable place for a family than crowded London. Their hearts became set to venture to the new world.

The Dyers sold their property and set sail in the late spring of 1635. The ocean voyage was a rugged initiation to what was to come: "stiff gales and stormy boisterous nights in which the sea rafted and tossed exceedingly." After ten weeks of stretching eyes towards an unadorned horizon, small shapes began to make their appearance. A receiving line of islands awaited them, thirty in all. Some were tree-tufted, others rock sharp, some sandy smooth, and others dazzling with fruits and flowers in bloom. Their inhabitants, predominantly deer, gazed in wonder at the big white sails approaching. Their ship, a brig, nosed the water smelling out the location of Boston. At last, that land appeared distinct behind the multitude of islands, a peninsula tethered to the mainland by a string of rocks. The Tri-Mountains — Pemberton, Beacon, and Mt. Vernon ' served as a background, the highest peak whittled by the wind to resemble the head of a man, overlooking the village snuggled amid modest fields and sparsely wooded areas. The shoreline was trimmed with marshes indented with inlets of water. God's chosen acres awaited their arrival — with many surprises.

Five months pregnant, Mary was overcome with gratitude for survival and the stillness of the land.

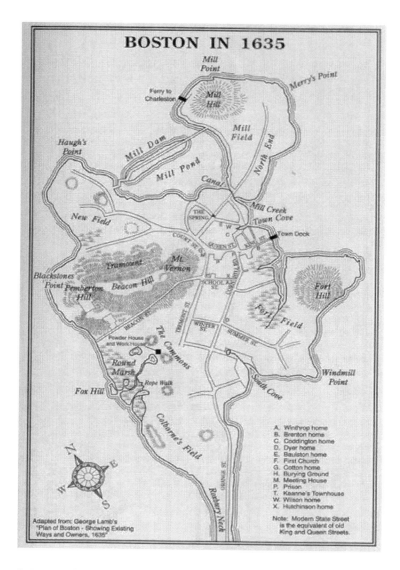

2. Boston in 1635 (drawn by Philip Schwartzberg.).

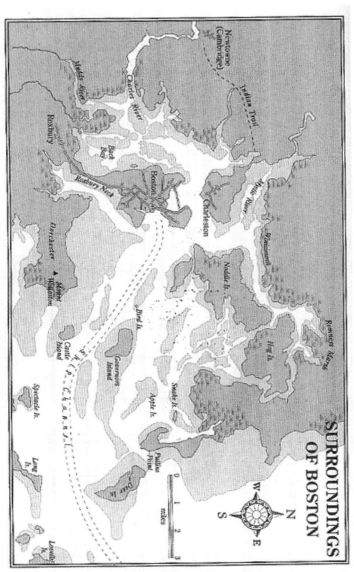

3.Surroundings of Boston (drawn by Philip Schwartzberg).

{ 3 }
Settling In

Wee must be knitt together in this work as one man, wee must entertaine each other in brotherly affection, wee must be willing to abridge ourselves of superfluities,"[1] professed John Winthrop from the deck of the Arabella in 1630. By the time the Dyers arrived in Boston in 1635, this statement had permeated the community and had become a way of life. Although Winthrop did not always hold the office of Governor, he was to remain the essential leader for Massachusetts Bay Colony until his death in 1649.

Mary Dyer first noticed that the houses were all clustered closely together despite ample surrounding space. Winthrop had ruled that all buildings should be within half-a-mile of the center of Boston, where he had his home.[2] Anyone who wished to live further away could found their own town, as happened in Roxbury, Newtowne (Cambridge), Wollaston, etc.[3]

The Dyers took possession of a lot on Summer Street, with just enough land for a house, garden and a few fruit saplings brought with them from England. As Massachusetts Bay Colony was a commercial enterprise, its Royal Charter provided land for stockholders like William Dyer, who had contributed fifty pounds as well as paying for the passage of his family and individual servants.[4]

Mary and William proceeded to build the house which was to be their nest. The nearby forest was replete with a variety of trees unlike anything William had ever seen in England. Felling such giant trees was a strenuous process and the builders found it more efficient to cut the planks in place, dividing the jobs between them so that some would saw, some rive, and others would carry the wood back to the building site.

The first builders were limited by the lack of adequate tools, particularly those needed to make the large fireplaces so central to every house. Although surrounded by an abundance of rocks, they did not have the tools required for chipping stones, and it took some time to develop kilns for the making of brick. The first fireplaces were made of wooden planks secured with mud. Combined with thatched roofs, the method created a tremendous fire hazard, for which every household was instructed to stand alert: leather buckets were always filled with water ready to respond instantly to the dreaded night calls of "Fire, fire!"[5]

The Dyer house was designed around a fireplace of such dimensions that seven foot logs were carried by horse and cart (or sled) directly from forest to hearth. The luxury of the resultant light and warmth compensated for the tiny windows covered with oiled linen. Flames brightened the whole living "hall", casting weird shadows on the ceiling of herbs dangling from the rafters. The Dyers slept in a room behind the fireplace while the indentured servants climbed a ladder to the loft above. Every night before retiring, William was careful to rake the coals in hopes they would hold their flicker till daybreak.

Although the pots and pans brought from England all hung on chains attached to a travel rod within the fireplace, there had not been room aboard their ship for bringing any furniture. William soon turned his skills to carpentry, first crafting a `settle', a high-backed bench, to protect them from winter draughts while sitting by the fireside. Then he shaped a long oak table called a "board," with the customary chair for the head of the family to sit at the end of the table, resulting in the title, "the chairman of the board." Mary and the rest of the family would sit on benches. What especially pleased Mary was the maple cradle, cleverly designed to be turned upside down when the baby grew older, with the rockers serving as arms for a little bench. Anticipation of birth was ever present.

Evenings were most often spent reading the Bible. All life was dependant on a careful knowledge of the Bible.

There were so many skills to acquire just to stay alive in this foreign land. William Dyer was not an experienced farmer, but he had the fortune to meet up with William Brenton, John Coggeshall and William Coddington, who had all brought a wealth of farming knowledge with them from England. The Dyers were among ten other families allotted 240 acres of land for farming and grazing cattle on Rommeys Marsh[6] and Pullens Point. From Pullens Point, one could see the hard-working fishermen who were often forced to beach their shallops and drag them across the land when neither sail nor oars could withstand the coercion of the wind and the tide. Thus the name "Pull-In Point." By land and by sea every man was challenged to provide enough food to keep the colony alive. They could not forget the first winter, when, on the edge of starvation, half of the settlers had died.

Every man had his own livelihood to attend to, but he was also expected to volunteer service for community projects. William Dyer was soon asked to lead such a group in constructing a fort on the hill to the south of Boston.[7] From Fort Hill one could overlook Boston Harbor and commandeer all shipping activities. For a more extensive view beyond the harbor and the multitude of islands out to sea, it was necessary to climb Beacon Hill, from which one could look way down the coast to be forewarned of any invaders, as well as to welcome ships coming from England. A large tub of tar lay on the peak of Beacon Hill, ready to be lit as a warning to the community of any approaching danger.

The multitude of potential dangers served to bond the Dyers with the rest of the community during the first months, while spiritual differences remained temporarily submerged.

The work assigned the women might have appeared to be devoid of the kind of adventure experienced by the men, but Mary had never plucked a goose before and the battle with the hooded squawking birds was a domestic challenge. Much was learned about the new life of total self-sufficiency, without too much time to ponder what Winthrop really intended by his covenant with God. For a short time, acceptance served as the crutch for an overwhelming life of domestic details. Like the men, the women also "knit together as one" for many of their assignments. "Whangs" of women went about cleaning one house at a time. Then there was "change work"--women gathered to churn quantities of apple butter, make rag rugs, or, most odious of all, boil their collected scraps of fat with quantities of ashes for the year's supply of soap. These working meetings gave Mary the chance to become acquainted with other wives, such as Dorothy Brenton, Mary Coggeshall, Elizabeth Aspinwall and Sarah Cotton. Of all her new acquaintances, she was most drawn to Anne Hutchinson. Anne and her husband, William, had come from Alford, England in 1633, with a family of eleven children. They lived in a large house on School Street across from Governor Winthrop. Anne was vivid, passionate, opinionated, and high-spirited. She moved around town with fire and purpose. Mary responded like lightning to her presence.

Every Sunday at 9:00 a.m., the drums would alert the community to proceed to the little mud church on the corner of Corn Hill Road and King Street. Attendance was compulsory and there was a fine for not attending the Congregational Church,[8] which was founded by John Winthrop and his followers in Boston. Mary put on her best skirt, blouse, jacket and hooded cape. William wore his leather britches belted to carry his revolver and bullets, as every man was expected to attend church armed; a guard stood at the door on watch for any Indian interlopers. Although Mary and William often walked down the street hand in hand, they knew that no expressions of affection were acceptable on Sunday. Outside the meeting house stood a whipping post and stocks as a reminder of the punishment waiting for anyone who disregarded any of the Puritan laws.

Once inside, Mary took her place with her foot-warmer on one side of the church with the women, while William joined the men on the other side. Very young children sat next to their mothers while older boys were kept in order by a tithing man at the back of the church.

The changes from the services of St. Martins-in-the-Field were dramatic and at first they gave a feeling of freedom to the Congregational Church. No candles were used, and sparse light filtered through the oil-papered windows. No altar. No music. The ruling elders and deacons, dressed in black and resembling learned lawyers, sat up front facing the congregation. After half an hour of psalms, John Wilson ascended the pulpit, with an hourglass to time his sermon.

John Wilson was thirty-two, a graduate of Kings College, Cambridge. Just after he started his first parish, John Winthrop asked him to be the minister for the Arabella. Wilson left his new parish reluctantly, for his wife refused to accompany him across the ocean. Once in Boston, he was elected preacher of the First Church, and as he had been ordained in England, he chose to continue the tradition of the succession of bishops, and refused to be re-ordained in Boston. This was in contrast to the First Congregational Church in America, started in 1628 in Salem, when their first ministers, Francis Higginson and Samuel Skelton, changed the Anglican practice of laying on of hands to maintain the succession of the minister of the church.

Like many of the other Puritan ministers forbidden to preach in England, Wilson was eager to make up for lost time. He would preach for the required hour and then turn over his hourglass so that the sands could fall with his words for another hour. There were no prayers after his sermon. John Winthrop and John Wilson had tossed all the Anglican prayer books overboard once the Arabella had left England. Prayers were composed by men and only the Bible contained the word of God. By dismissing the form and elegance of the Church of England in an attempt to return to the simplicity of the Apostles, the Boston Church was not necessarily rediscovering the truth for a woman like Mary Dyer. However, as Mary sat listening to Wilson's preaching, it could not have occurred to her that this austere man would play a critical role in her life.

After a short break at noon for warmth and food, Mary returned to hear the teacher of the Church, John Cotton. The afternoon service must have been more rewarding than the morning for Mary Dyer because, while Wilson had preached the moral law, Cotton preached the spirit, emphasizing absolute faith, rather than conduct, as important. Every Congregational Church had a teacher, as well as a preacher, and it was the function of Cotton as "teacher" to expound and maintain the purity of the doctrine. Cotton spent twelve hours a day studying to prepare himself for this assignment. A graduate of Trinity College, Cambridge, ordained at Emmanuel, and Vicar at St. Botolph's in Boston, Lincolnshire, Cotton had been very popular with his parishioners but was discounted as a non-conformist by the bishops of the Anglican Church. When he was discharged from office in 1633, his thoughts turned towards New England. As a friend of John Winthrop and John Wilson, he had given the farewell sermon on the decks of the Arabella when they departed from England. Sarah Cotton, in contrast to John Wilson's wife, was not only eager to accompany her husband to Boston on board the Griffin, but gave birth, mid-ocean, to a son they called Seaborne Cotton.

After Cotton's sermon, the congregation was expected to stay on into the early evening attending to church business. It was a long day in a damp, unheated meeting house. The Thursday meeting was shorter, followed by a marketing day in the square next to the First Church, attended by people from all the outlying towns. The gathering place was at Robert Keayne's, a transplanted London tradesman who had great plans for making Boston like London. His tavern grew into the first Boston Town House. It was Keayne's desire to combine a shelter "for the country people who come with their provisions ... to sitt dry and warme both in cold raine and durty weather" with a "conveniant room or two for the Courts to meet in" and a "roome for a Library and a gallery or some other handsome rooms for the elders to meet in and confer together, as well as an armory for the Artillery Company" " all built on pillars so that "the open roome between the pillairs may serve for merchants, Master of Ship and Strangers as well as the towne " to meet in."[9] Mary would join the other women in examining the latest goods from England. The smallest nail or needle from London shone like silver in Boston. Prices were controlled by the magistrates with no opportunity left for free enterprise.

The most important thing in Boston was to belong to the Congregational Church. Mere attendance was not sufficient. An interview was required with Preacher John Wilson. It was essential to relate a religious experience that would convince him of one's qualifications to be considered a regenerate Christian. Next came interviews with the elders, and finally with the congregation. Mary Dyer had to respond to many searching questions about her religious experiences. When Sarah Cotton came up for membership three years before, John Cotton tried to change the ruling, feeling that it would be more modest and suitable for women to be interviewed in private. The Congregation protested, saying that women should undergo the same testing as men. After days of examination, on December 13, 1635, Mary and William Dyer became members of the Boston Congregational Church, confirming with handshakes the "right hand of fellowship" with all the other Congregationalists. As members of the Church, the men were given the right to vote for the ministers and elders as well as the acceptance or expulsion of Church members. It must have felt peculiar to Mary to undergo the same questioning and examination as William without enjoying the privilege of the vote. However, she was allowed to partake in communion, which was important to her.[10]

The timing of the reception of the Dyers into the First Church of Boston on December 13th was fortunate. On December 20th, a healthy son, named Samuel, was born to Mary and William Dyer. In order to "wash away original sin," a child had to be baptized within twenty-four hours of birth. Only the offspring of Church members were eligible for baptism. Samuel made it by one week. However, he would not qualify as an "elect" adult by baptism alone; like all the other baptized children, he would have to be examined, as his parents had been, when he became of age.

Membership in the Congregational Church qualified the men to become "freemen." It was the unique requirement for citizenship in the colony. William was now a candidate, but not, of course, Mary, who was legally mute, without any opportunity to express any opinion on anything that mattered, as women and servants were excluded from any participation in political affairs. It was customary for the men to be interviewed by the Governor and Magistrates to qualify as responsible members of the community. Participation in the Commonwealth, which was limited to voting for officers, was contingent on belonging to the Church. It was a compact of consent between the rulers and the ruled, with the belief that the government was really appointed by God through the people. The knot was tightly tied between Church and State.

After three months of interviews and meeting with the authorities, William Dyer became a freeman on March 3, 1636. The Dyers could now rejoice that they at last belonged. As in the Church, William had the power to vote for the officers but could not make decisions for the community.

Both Mary and William were eager to learn the law of the land, expecting it to reflect the common law of England. But this was not the case. Puritan law was taken from the Old Testament, as interpreted by the magistrates and ministers of the colony. It was sometimes hard to read by the dwindling evening fire, and it would take many months to gather enough tallow for dipping candles. The Dyers were happy to learn how the Indians split pine faggots, which released quantities of turpentine and pitch to create torches even brighter than candles.

William had never had any legal training, but he learned in Boston that the legislative power lay in a general court. If no law covered a situation, one was written as near as possible to the law of God, with scripture providing authorization. Winthrop believed the Bible could be made the rule of life. The clergy prepared the first draft of such laws, so that, in effect, the civil authority derived from the church. Anyone breaking any one of the Ten Commandments was punishable by death.[11] William found it was hard to discover what laws the colony had set down, for Winthrop had objected to their codification, fearing some principles might run counter to the English law. The Royal Charter stated that no law should be "repugnant to England" and John Winthrop wanted to appear loyal to England. The best way to learn the laws of the Colony was to listen to Preacher Wilson every Sunday and Thursday. His sermons contained direct political instructions. It was clear that the Church and the State were performing as one.

It took almost a year for Mary and William to feel established in Winthrop's "City on the Hill", building their home, planting the crops, tending the animals, fulfilling the qualifications of belonging to the Church and State, and getting to know the other people.

Winthrop's concept of "being knit together as one" had great appeal at first. It was not until they began to feel the tightness of the knitting that Mary and William became aware of the constraints.

Mary and William made a practice of pausing for a moment on their settle in front of the fire at the end of each strenuous day to exchange the reactions of two very independent minds, an unusual custom in the male-dominated world in which they lived. Positioned on the windward side of privilege, they delayed their realization of the deprivations of the majority; but soon they could not help but observe the unfortunate results of Winthrop's most radical interpretation of God's design for the universe. With a dramatic singleness of purpose, Winthrop told his followers that all men must accept the place in society in which they found themselves: "Some must be rich, some poore, some high and eminent in power and dignitie, and others meane and in subjeccion," all standing in need of one another.[12] The word of God as expressed in the Bible was to be the one source of inspiration, and guide to everyday living. As they were under a covenant with God, there could be only one religion. That any other should be tolerated would be an insult to God. This message reflected the influence of John Calvin of Geneva, who was the spokesman throughout Europe for the idea that there was a covenant of mutual obligation between God and man, that man's fate was predestined and only the elect could be saved.

For a society where religion was for everybody the one most absorbing and all-consuming factor in life, the act of exclusion, from what mattered most, must have been devastating.

Mary saw that of all the people who had left their homes in England and risked the voyage for a more democratic life, less than half were eligible for any privileges; the majority were not permitted to partake in communion or baptism services, nor were they qualified to be freemen. Without being able to vote in church or state affairs they were like spiritual non-entities in the community. England's oligarchy had not been left behind.

4. This Meeting House was used for civic and religious meetings until the Congregational Church was built.(Courtesy of Boston Athenaeum)

5. Keayne's Town House (courtesy of Boston Athenaeum).

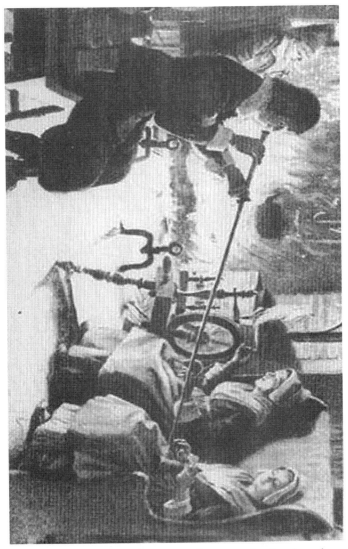

6. The Whispering Rod--means of communicating love in a crowded room (courtesy of Bettmann Archive).

7. Portrait of John Winthrop by O. Pelton (courtesy of
Boston Public Library).

{ 4 }
Unsettling

As Mary and William Dyer were just beginning to feel their way into the life of Massachusetts Bay Colony during the fall-winter of 1635-36, they became aware of great disturbances amongst the magistrates and ministers. John Haynes, the Governor of the year, was a man of substance who had arrived with John Cotton two years earlier. In another two years he would leave Massachusetts to become the first chosen Governor of Connecticut. As Governor of Massachusetts Bay Colony in 1635, he was under considerable strain. William Dyer soon discovered that it was Roger Williams who was responsible for the general unease. John Winthrop loved Roger and often referred to his "magnificent stride." But Roger had strode through Boston, Salem, and Plymouth like a bull in a china shop. He had foregone the possibility of being the preacher for the Boston Church in 1633 because of his opinion that the only way to express freedom of religion was to break away completely from the Church of England. Governor John Winthrop had no intention of severing connections with the Anglican Church; he simply wished to revise and improve its ways.

Just before Roger Williams passed up the opportunity to be the preacher of the Boston Church, Francis Higginson died of tuberculosis. The symbolic separation from the Anglican Church, Higginson had made by being ordained by the Salem congregation was enough to satisfy Roger Williams for the time being. When Williams was offered the position of preacher to replace Francis Higginson, he gladly accepted and moved from Boston to Salem[1] where he was living when the Dyers arrived in Boston.

Roger Williams was scheduled to appear before the Massachusetts

General Court in December to account for all the "dangerous opinions" he had been preaching to the people of Salem and Plymouth, which had caused much discussion outside the Church and around the marketplace.

Roger Williams' ideas concerned the colonists' right to own land, which he felt belonged to the Indians. Mary and William Dyer were happy with their allotment of land, with the little garden behind their house already planted with vegetables and herbs, as well as the added acreage on Pullens Point and Romneys Marsh for the grazing of cattle and growing of grains. Their ownership of land gave them a great sense of belonging.

Roger Williams had become involved in the lives of the Indians around Salem and Plymouth and had become concerned over their rights to the land they had occupied before the arrival of the colonists. Roger maintained that any land which had not been purchased by the white man belonged to the Indian. It was illegal simply to take it over. The Indians were an independent tribe and in no way could they be considered subject to England. This view became a bone of contention between him and Governor Winthrop and the Boston authorities. Governor Winthrop argued that the Charter had given them permission to claim any land which was not already inhabited. It was his opinion that the Indians had not settled on any one piece of land. They were like nomads, always on the move, transporting their homes from farming land in summer to fishing banks in winter. While Winthrop questioned how one could call such wanderers landowners, Roger continued to accuse the English of stealing land from the Indians. Mary and William had not had the same opportunity as Roger to associate with Indians, because many of the Massachusetts tribe, living on the outskirts of Boston, had died of disease.

Although the Dyers were new and untried in the community they could not dismiss Roger's feelings about separation of Church and State. Roger always turned to the Bible in his attempt to seek its truth. As he reread the Ten Commandments, it suddenly occurred to him that the first four commandments addressed man's relationship with God and therefore belonged to the Church. The last six commandments concerned man's relationship to man and therefore were subject to the laws of the state. Roger Williams referred to the first four as Table One and the last six as Table Two. He thought magistrates should not have the authority to punish men for such sins as not appearing at church on Sunday, a Table One transgression, but they should only judge and be able to punish the breaking of the commandments of the second Table, those that referred to relationships between people. This clear separation of the functions of Church and State struck Mary and William Dyer as reasonable. It appeared suicidal to the Boston authorities who felt the death penalty should be the punishment for breaking any one of the Ten Commandments.

During his first months, William Dyer had taken the residents' oath of loyalty to Massachusetts Bay Colony, which had replaced the former church oath. William was still glad to do anything that showed he belonged to the new colony. Roger Williams, on the other hand, refused to take the oath[2]. It was his strong conviction that oaths were a sacred experience between man and God; never between man and man. Roger's views made William Dyer think twice about the oaths he had already taken.

Roger Williams was called before the Massachusetts General Court in July 1635. Thomas Hooker engaged Roger in a formal debate on his opinions.[3] As he did not deny any of the charges against him, there was no need for a trial. In October 1635, the General Court met again, with John Haynes still Governor. The eight assistants were several of Roger's old Essex friends: William Coddington, Simon Bradstreet, Thomas Dudley, John Wilson, and John Winthrop. Two or three deputies were chosen from the freemen of each town. One at a time, each man walked into the meeting house and placed his vote on the table: a kernel of corn signified a positive vote and a bean registered negative. The sentence of banishment was passed with only one opposing vote.[4] No surviving record indicates which loyal friend dropped the green bean. Roger was given six weeks to leave the Colony.

When Roger returned to Salem, he was excluded from the Church. Plenty of devoted parishioners were ready to follow him to his home for meetings. When word trickled back to Boston that the people of Salem were congregating in Roger's house, Governor Haynes and his magistrates feared conspiracy. They decided that more immediate action was necessary to get rid of Roger and the safest plan would be to send him back to England.

Governor Haynes ordered Captain John Underhill to sail to Salem and pick him up. Captain Underhill brought his pinnace into the cove of Salem and proceeded to the Williams' home. He knocked on the door and presently was met by Mary Williams, carrying her newborn baby, Freeborn, in one arm, followed by her toddler Mary, who had fast hold on her skirt. Captain Underhill asked for Roger Williams. He was not at home. How long had he been gone? Mary replied, "Three days." Where had he gone? Mary was truthful in answering that she did not know. Captain Underhill departed without satisfaction; the culprit had fled.

This news astounded Boston. The Dyers were particularly upset; Mary Dyer was concerned about Mary Williams being deserted in Salem with her two little daughters; William Dyer feared that he might never see Roger Williams again. They had no way of knowing what good fortune Roger's sudden flight would bring them.

{ 5 }
Hutchinsonians Become Antinomians

It started at the spring that glorious source of fresh water which had prompted John Winthrop to transfer the original settlement from Charlestown to Boston in 1629. As it was women's work to fetch the water, bucket by bucket, day after day, the spring became their natural meeting place. Every morning Mary Dyer would walk up Corn Hill Road looking for the jaunty figure of Anne Hutchinson swinging her buckets as she side-stepped the multitude of muddy puddles. Grabbing her pail, Mary would run to catch up with Anne. As Mary and Anne sauntered along together, conversation passed between them like a fresh gushing stream. Religion was the main topic, in particular the sermons of John Wilson in which he reiterated, Sunday after Sunday, the theme of "salvation by work" and his insistence that God's total message to mankind could be found in the Old Testament. There was no justification for looking any further. Anne believed that those rules were written for another people at another time. She believed in "salvation by grace," and in the inspirational messages of love, joy, and service to mankind found in the New Testament. Her appealing advice was to get your heart ready and you cannot sin! It was Anne's opinion that salvation was not earned by conduct, obeying the Commandments, giving alms, praying, fasting or wearing a long face; all that implied a mere "covenant of works." Such things were good in themselves but they did not prove the state of one's heart. A serene spirit, coming from the consciousness of God's state within, proves the true believer that he is among the elect. Anne Hutchinson's message was exuberant.

"He in whom the spirit swells is of the elect."

When Mary Dyer heard Anne Hutchinson express these sentiments, her spirit swelled. She began to realize that she had not crossed the Atlantic Ocean for what was being taught in the Boston Church, but for the inspirational talks with Anne Hutchinson.

Other women who frequented the spring became interested in joining the lively conversations of Anne Hutchinson and Mary Dyer. Dorothy Brenton, Mary Coggeshall, and Sarah Cotton would all linger on the banks of the spring waiting for the appearance of Anne and Mary to discuss the Sunday morning preaching of John Wilson as well as the Sunday afternoon teaching of John Cotton. Anne Hutchinson seemed so knowledgeable in understanding and so gifted in explaining the complicated monologues of the men. Anne deplored the views of John Wilson but was radiant with praise for the words of John Cotton. She confessed that he was her sole reason for coming to New England. In Alford, she had been so put off by the preaching she heard, that she had become an agnostic. Anne confided that she had experienced a vision in which God told her to listen to John Cotton. He quickly became her idol, and when he left England to join Winthrop in New England, Anne persuaded her whole family to follow him.

The women gathered at the spring listened intently and confessed that they did not altogether understand what Cotton was saying. Anne suggested that these women might meet at her home on Mondays to discuss the Sunday sermons, and seek a greater understanding together. Anne could answer any questions about the Bible convincingly, though she did not have the benefit of the formal religious education, which was only available to men.

The next Monday, Mary Dyer joined three other women to meet at the Hutchinson's house, where Anne volunteered an explanation of the Sunday sermon. When other women heard about this gathering they wanted to come too. Every Monday, a group met at Anne's house and each week the numbers increased, the rapidly growing membership reflecting the great need among the women of Boston, not only for clarifications of religious subjects, but for diversion from their relentless chores.

Mondays in the Hutchinson house were a contrast to Sundays in the Boston Church; Mary noticed a difference in the other women approaching Anne's house, their stiff, somber faces transformed by happy expressions. A huge fire blazed in the Hutchinson's brick fireplace. Patterns of sunlight found entrance through the imported English glass windows, and bright curtains advertised the fact that William Hutchinson had choice materials for sale around the corner. The warm atmosphere and the sharing of exhilarating ideas put people at their ease. Such an exchange of ideas would have been unthinkable, unallowable, at the Boston Church.

Mary Dyer was eager for William to partake of this new experience. She wondered how he would react. William listened intently as Mary told him Anne's ideas about the difference between a "covenant of work" and a "covenant of grace." He was silent for a while, and then he surprised Mary with a question that made her very happy, asking if he might even attend these meetings. William's participation, in what seemed to be her separate world, brought a synthesis to the edges of her life, as well as a supreme moment of togetherness to their marriage. William led the way and other husbands were encouraged to join the women's group.

Many of the men, like William Brenton, John Coggeshall, and William Coddington were merchants who had become discouraged by the lack of opportunity for private enterprise in Boston. Religious beliefs and restrictions curbed the freedom of trade. In this new world, so inspiring for individual pursuits, the concept of John Winthrop's community was inhibiting. It was at Anne Hutchinson's meetings that the disappointed merchants gathered new hope for the possibilities of individual enterprise in every sphere of life. Anne was gathering more and more followers among the men. One of the most enthusiastic was Harry Vane.

A few months before Roger Williams vanished into the wilderness, a dashing young man wearing a black cape over a scarlet vest, stepped onto the Massachusetts shore, fresh from a theological school in Geneva. Harry Vane was twenty-four years old, young enough to be John Winthrop's son, and bursting with the exuberance of a younger generation. His non-conformist attitudes had been of great concern and embarrassment to his father, Sir Henry Vane, who was on the privy council of the court of King Charles I. Father and King devised a solution by sending young Harry on a trip to New England. John Winthrop was deputy governor at the time of Vane's arrival and felt honor-bound to give a gracious welcome to this well-connected young man, but his overwhelming popularity soon posed a real problem for Winthrop[1]. Vane was an old friend of the Dyers. Mary had known him at Buckingham Palace.

Harry Vane brought a special sparkle to Anne's meetings, which served to increase the number of followers. Soon the original five members increased to about 80 people. The Hutchinson house became so crowded that the overflow had to stand on School Street and lean in the open windows, and it soon became necessary to schedule a second meeting on Thursdays to take care of the popular demand.

John Winthrop, John Wilson, Thomas Dudley, and Simon Bradstreet were conspicuous in their absence from the Hutchinson house. Governor Winthrop could peer out his window, tugging his black triangular beard, and angrily watch the people filling the doors and windows across the street to hear the woman he had described in his journal as one with a "haughty carriage, of a nimble wit, an active spirit, and a voluble tongue, more than any man, though in understanding and judgment inferior to a woman." Undoubtedly he had his wife, Margaret, in mind as a "superior woman."

Winthrop was very concerned about the influence of Anne Hutchinson on all those other women, especially Mary Dyer, who he considered "a very prompt and a very fair woman of a very proud spirit."[2] He wanted her to fall in line as one of his followers, but she continued to act like a deputy of Anne Hutchinson's.

At another window, Margaret Winthrop could peek between the curtains and also observe the gathering of women, watching all the other women cross the street to join the meeting. Margaret was most interested in observing Anne Hutchinson and Mary Dyer, because they were the women who had visited her time and time again during her many periods of ill health, stopping to call when she was most depressed and lightening her world with "buoyant words, healing herbs, and cordials." As midwives, they had assisted her through many obstetrical difficulties. Margaret Winthrop must have longed to drop her knitting and reach out to the expressed happiness across the street, but her great love for her Governor demanded obedience.

Anne Dudley Bradstreet, wife of the Magistrate (and later Governor) Simon Bradstreet, and daughter of the Magistrate (and the sometimes Governor) Thomas Dudley, was another sensitive woman denied permission to mingle with the Hutchinson group. Her hopes, joys and frustrations found expression in her poetry. Our first American poetess. To Winthrop's objection that no woman allow herself any diversion from her duties as a housewife, Anne Bradstreet responded:

> I am obnoxious to each carping tongue
> Who say my hand a needle better fits.
> A poet's pen all scorn I should thus wrong,
> For such despite they cast on Female wits;
> If what I do prove well, it won't advance,
> They'l say it's stol'n, or else it was by chance.[3]

People everywhere were taking sides on the religious issues. Even small children were caught up in the religious ferment. They went around asking one another, "Are your parents for 'grace' or "works?" Most of them did not understand the significance of the questions but they answered anyway.[4]

William Dyer was as involved as Mary in taking the religious pulse of the community. Crossing the Charles River by ferry, he was pleased to hear the ferryman, Thomas Marshall, discuss the importance of "salvation by grace," encouraging his passengers to join him and Dyer at the meetings at Anne Hutchinson's house. Another opportunist was the barber-surgeon, William Dyneley. As William Dyer sat waiting to have his hair cut the required length above the shoulders and below the ears, he listened to Dyneley advocating "salvation by grace" with every razor's stroke.

In the ferry, at the barbers and at William Baulston's tavern — everywhere people were discussing the same topic: "salvation by works" versus "salvation by grace." William Baulston was another member of Anne Hutchinson's extended meetings. For every glass of ale he poured, he reminded his customers that the spirit was "grace." "Bottoms up to Mrs. Hutchinson!" he would call out. Everywhere it was "Bottoms up to Mrs. Hutchinson." She was becoming the most sought after person in the community, to the utter delight of Mary Dyer and the utter dismay of Governor Winthrop.

Governor Winthrop asserted that the Hutchinsonians "bred disturbance in civil affairs." However, he took some comfort in the realization that women were not eligible for office. Anne Hutchinson could never be a magistrate, minister, or even a freeman. There was no way she could vote, but she could not be stopped from trying to project her ideas into a world of masculine power. The debate between "works" and "faith" was escalating. Which group was eligible for Heaven? Would bitter repentance or joyful generosity qualify as the passport? The member of the Hutchinsonian group who worried Winthrop the most was Harry Vane. His exuberant personality helped many Bostonians turn to "salvation by grace" and away from Winthrop's "salvation by work." Winthrop's greatest fear became a reality on May 25, 1636, when all the ships in the harbor sent off rockets to celebrate Harry Vane's election as Governor of Massachusetts Bay Colony. For ex-Governor John Winthrop this was a disaster. His disapproval increased as Vane, accustomed to all the pomp and circumstance of the British court, named four sergeants to serve as his honor guards.

The day after Harry Vane's election, Anne Hutchinson's brother-in-law, John Wheelwright, arrived in Boston. He was a minister and a great favorite of Anne's. Wheelwright came at a time when the Hutchinsonians were beginning to feel the need for a representative to counteract the influence of John Wilson in the Boston Church. Governor Harry Vane was quick to support this plan to have John Wheelwright step in as third minister. Deputy Governor Winthrop and Preacher Wilson foresaw the potential conflict and arranged for Wheelwright to take the Wollaston Church instead. This rejection of Wheelwright became the chief topic of Anne Hutchinson's meetings, and Winthrop the target of their attack.

Winthrop dreaded any sort of fanaticism. Nothing could be more threatening to the Colony than to have Anne Hutchinson believing that God spoke directly to her. He was anxious for the reputation of the Colony and fearful that their dispute would be reported back to England. King Charles I had already threatened withdrawal of the Royal Charter. As a result of these fears, the Hutchinsonians were tagged "Antinomians" by the Boston magistrates.

The term "Antinomian" is derived from the Greek, "anti nominos," meaning against and opposed to the law. The title was coined by Martin Luther who applied it to the adherents of John Agricola, who disregarded the law in expressing his belief that the followers of the Mosaic law were unregenerate and the only true Christians were the followers of the Gospel. The Hutchinsonians differed, in that they had no intention of destroying the Boston Church, but they felt qualified to improve it. Their "covenant of grace" maintained that a life of spontaneous and loving service was a more important preparation for salvation than repentance and fast days. And when, in time, the Hutchinsonians were tagged Antinomians, the tension increased dramatically.

Anne Hutchinson claimed that the only two ministers in the Colony who were worth listening to were Wheelwright and Cotton. They alone preached the "covenant of grace." All the rest preached a "covenant of works." The slandered ministers pleaded with Anne for recognition and planned a meeting at John Cotton's house to discuss the issues with her. In October 1636, Anne's only supporters among the assembly of ministers were John Wheelwright, John Cotton, and Thomas Leverett, along with Governor Vane attending as her most ardent follower. The challenging opponents were John Wilson of Boston, Thomas Shepherd of Newtowne, Hugh Peters of Salem, Thomas Weld of Roxbury, Zachary Symnes of Charlestown, and George Phillips of Watertown. They asked Anne outright whether she believed that all the ministers except for Cotton and Wheelwright were unfit to preach. She gave an elusive answer: "You can preach no more than you know." Her reply insinuated that the ministers who were at the core of the colony were unfit to preach. It was unforgivable slander. As dissension mounted, they called for a "day of fasting and humiliation" to repress the "divers opinions of the colony." The time was ripe for an event to clarify the issues.

Mary Dyer was at Anne Hutchinson's side as she discussed the possibilities of bringing her brother-in-law, John Wheelwright, back from Wollaston to be visiting preacher at the Boston Church. When John Wilson decided to return to England to try and persuade his reluctant wife to join him in Boston, they realized that the moment had come for Cotton to invite Wheelwright as a guest speaker at the Sunday service.

It was a bitterly cold day on January 20, 1637. John Wheelwright trudged through the snow from Wollaston to the Boston Church where he met John Cotton. It was agreed that Cotton would speak at the morning service and Wheelwright would preach in the afternoon. Wheelwright's Fast Day Sermon startled everyone. He started off by saying that those who practiced a "covenant of works" were "enemies of Christ." It was his figures of speech that shook the congregation. He shouted his message, "We must kill them with the work of the Lord — We must all prepare for a spiritual combat." He pounded the pulpit and continued, "We must put on the whole arms of God. We must be ready to fight. We must all prepare for battle and come against our enemy."[5] His metaphor was taken quite literally and interpreted as a threat of outright sedition. Mary Dyer clenched the bench beneath her as she listened to Wheelwright's "war cry" — she glanced in the direction of Anne Hutchinson. Her face was lit with excitement and her head was nodding in approval. At the end of the service most parishioners were trembling with emotion as well as cold, as they left the Boston Church. Winthrop was whiter than the snow. He feared civil war.

John Wheelwright was accused of contempt and sedition before a closed court; the freemen were denied their right to be present. He was given two weeks to leave Massachusetts Bay Colony. Anne Hutchinson's followers met in fury over the fate of her brother-in-law. He tried to appeal to King Charles I but was forbidden access by the Boston magistrates. William Aspinwall drew up a petition suggesting that Wheelwright was not guilty of contempt or sedition. The petition also recommended that the hearings on Wheelwright be open to the public. Sixty freemen, consisting of the majority of the Boston Church, signed the petition. As women, neither Anne Hutchinson nor Mary Dyer was allowed to sign. The excitement continued for four months. The petition was to be voted on at the May session of the General Court. John Wilson had returned from England, finally accompanied by his reluctant wife, Elizabeth. John Cotton, who had been wavering between the establishment and the Antinomians, was beginning to be swayed over on the side of the other ministers, much to the amazement and consternation of Anne Hutchinson and Mary Dyer. However, with Harry Vane still holding the office of Governor, the Hutchinsonians felt confident. The agenda was all-important. All the freemen could vote to elect the Governor and Magistrates, but only those in office could vote on Aspinwall's petition. With this in mind, Governor Vane shrewdly arranged to have the people vote on the petition before the election. Winthrop was not to be so easily outsmarted. It was four years since he had been Governor and he wanted desperately to get back in the seat of power. He was very apprehensive about Vane's popularity in Boston. It occurred to him that if they moved the location of the General Court across the Charles River to Newtowne (Cambridge) it would be impossible for all the Vane enthusiasts to attend.

Boston and Newtowne were separated by a broad arm of the sea, forming the Charles River, and adjoining flats and marshes through which a canal had been dug. With flood tides and favorable breezes sometimes one could sail by way of Boston Neck through Roxbury and Watertown to the rivulet which led right into the town of Newtowne. The ferryman, Tom Marshall, had a scow outfitted with both sail and oars. This was the best approach in warm weather. When the marshes were frozen over in winter, the other possible course was the ferry from Long Wharf to Charlestown, with a walk through the woods from Charlestown to Newtowne.

It was a short walk for Mary and William to the Town Dock. They had to wait for the returning ferry. Finally, they spotted Thomas Marshall rowing with all his might to make up for the lost time. Weary from so much rowing back and forth with passengers from Roxbury and Duxbury, as well as Boston, he confided in the Dyers that he did not think that Vane stood a chance of holding office. The mood had changed.

As Mary and William approached the Newtowne green, they became aware of a crowd of excited people gathered around a large oak tree. Mary nudged William as they drew closer. She could hardly believe what she saw perched on one of the upper branches. Like a large crow, John Wilson, in black attire, was addressing the people. He cawed and cawed, "Election first, consult your charter!" He won his point. Moving over to one corner of the green, the magistrates and freemen gathered to vote. William Dyer could see he was in the minority. The majority of Boston inhabitants were for Vane, but the outlying towns voted for Winthrop. Not only did Winthrop replace Vane as Governor, but all of Anne's supporters lost their positions. Without office, the Hutchinsonians were helpless. Governor Winthrop and his counsel voted against the petition and Wheelwright was declared seditious. It was then decided that his punishment would be deferred until the meeting of the November Court.

Anne's son, Edward Hutchinson, was a member of Governor Vane's honor guard along with William Baulston. After the election, they threw down their halberds and made a dramatic exit with Vane, leaving Winthrop unescorted.

Mary and William Dyers' hopes and dreams had also tumbled to the ground. Thomas Marshall rowed them solemnly down the Newtowne inlet and across the Back-bay flats. The peninsula of Boston lay aglow reflecting the setting sun. Mary realized how attached she was becoming to its shape. As they approached the Roxbury marshes, skeins of geese were flushed up, instantly winging into perfect formation silhouetted against the evening twilight. Mary watched the geese as they kept shifting designs. How could they keep changing their pattern of flight with such ease and grace, and united sense of direction'?

8. Harry Vane, engraved by I. Swaine after a portrait
by Peter Lely (courtesy of New York Public Library).

{ 6 }
Pain of Birth

For Mary Dyer and her Antinomian friends, the summer of 1637 proved to be the antithesis of the golden year of 1636. In August all the congregational churches of Massachusetts held their first synod. For three weeks they conversed. And what was the concerted decision? Toleration for any form of worship other than Winthrop's was out of the question.

The once-exuberant Harry Vane became disgusted and depressed with all that was happening in Boston. Without office, he lost popularity. In two years he had witnessed the best and worst of the Massachusetts Bay Colony. In August 1637 he was ready to return to England. Although Governor Winthrop had suffered the presence of Vane as an acting figurehead in the Antinomian controversy, on Vane's departure, Winthrop wrote in his journal that Harry Vane "showed himself a true friend to New England and a man of noble and generous mind."

For Mary Dyer, the departure meant an end to all her hopes.

Although it was the most brilliant day in October, with every maple tree lighting up the town of Boston with color Mary felt her body was opposing this celebration of fall. She was going to have another child in December, one just two years younger than their son Samuel. Mary did not feel well. After several hours of cramps and increasing contractions she realized that she had gone into early labor, and called for a neighbor to alert her good friend Anne Hutchinson to come to her side.

Anne Hutchinson was an experienced midwife, who had learned by following the instructions of her mother in delivering her younger siblings. She could not have been an obstetrician without learning Latin, and such educational opportunities were only available to men.

But, aided by prayer and herbs, Anne had delivered many Boston babies. Her services were praised by John Cotton, who admitted, "Anne Hutchinson did much good in our town in woman's meetings and at childbirth travail, wherein she was not only skillful and helpful, but really fell in good discussion with women."

Another midwife who accompanied Anne on many Boston deliveries was Jane Hawkins, also called Goody Hawkins. She had come from St. Ives near Huntington and was known as a rhyming preacher who claimed direct revelation from God. As a prophetess, she had predicted the eventual downfall of all the bishops of the Anglican Church. While delivering babies she mixed ants, spider-webs and other peculiar objects of superstition with the healing herbs. Her practices suggested witchcraft and she was regarded with some suspicion in Boston, but as a follower of Anne Hutchinson her oddities were tolerated.

When news reached Anne that Mary was in labor she came running, with Goody Hawkins at her heels. They found Mary in the back room lying on her four-posted bed with the curtains parted and quilt askew. Anne had brought an assortment of herbs: basil for speedy delivery of a woman in labor, dill to hasten the milk, and mugwort for the afterbirth.

At first Mary tried to restrain herself, but she was overcome with pain and realized that her body must be contracting for birth. For hours she groaned and writhed. Anne felt out the baby, with her experienced touch, and decided it was turned the wrong way.[1] This was going to be a difficult delivery. Mary pushed for hours, with no avail, and finally fainted from the pain and exhaustion. Eventually, her body gave forth the child. There was not a sound. Anne examined the dead little girl. So many things had gone wrong. The child had a face, but no skull. For the moment, it was fortunate that Mary was not conscious to observe all the deformities of their newborn.

Anne held out the unfortunate little mishap for William Dyer to hold. He knew he must or he would never forgive himself. William found it hard to believe that anything so ugly could have resulted from their love for one another. For a moment, he must be father and mother to his dead deformed daughter.

William agreed with Anne that this birth must remain a secret in Boston. Governor Winthrop, John Wilson and the other magistrates and ministers were out looking for any faults they could find in their Antinomian opponents. The birth of a deformed dead child could easily be interpreted by the Governor as God's punishment against those who had challenged Winthrop's views. William understood that if their tragedy did not remain private, Mary would be personally blamed for the malformed baby. He suggested that they bury the dead child as quickly as possible.

Anne knew that English law permitted a midwife to bury a child in private. But in Massachusetts a midwife could not lawfully deliver or bury a child in secret because of a law created to police any attempts at abortion. Other Massachusetts laws prohibited a midwife to kill, maim or baptize. The Boston magistrates did not trust the women on whom their wives so frantically depended.

In her desperation as to what to do, Anne Hutchinson called on her old friend, John Cotton. Although he had betrayed her politically, she felt she could still call on him as a friend in a crisis.

John Cotton saw how this unfortunate birth could play into the hands of the Boston magistrates and ministers, and advised Anne to conceal it and bury it secretly. Mary was still unconscious. William elected to stay with her while Anne, Goody Hawkins, and John Cotton bundled the dead baby in an available sheet and walked nervously towards the graveyard of the Boston Church. It was late at night, and they only passed a few people along the way. They were particularly wary of meeting the night watchmen, who were often magistrates, marching two by two to patrol the streets of Boston. Although John Cotton felt anonymous in the night shadows, he knew that the distinctive pattern of light from his lantern formed a signature anyone could recognize. Every man's lantern was perforated by a different design, which served to identify the owner in the dark.

Anne stood alert at the graveyard gate as John Cotton pressed his shovel into the resistant earth. She felt a strange sense of partnership with this man with whom she had argued so bitterly in the recent weeks. John Cotton spaded up the earth with a recollection of the

English law in mind: "If any child shall be dead born, you yourself shall see it buried in such secret place as neither hog nor dog, nor any other beast come into it."

October 17, 1637, was a day that Mary Dyer was not allowed to forget.

{ 7 }
Trials

Mary had three weeks to recover her strength before attending the November General Court. John Wheelwright was accused of "constructive sedition," as a result of his Fast Day Sermon. Anne Hutchinson was to be tried "for traducing the ministers' and many of the Antinomian followers were up for judgment, including William Dyer. Mary Dyer knew her husband would be one of the first to be tried.

It was a sub-zero day in Boston on November 7, 1637. The snow had been falling for four days and lay "a yard deep." "This day it did snow two hours together (after much rain from the northeast) with flakes as great as shillings."[1] The Charles River was frozen solid from Boston to Newtowne, its banks heaped with layers of ice. Governor Winthrop had taken political advantage of the bitter weather and moved the location of the General Court from Boston to Newtowne, again thinking this inconvenience would reduce the attendance of the Boston core of Antinomians, knowing that the ferryman would not be able to transport the entire Boston population from Boston to Charlestown.

It was about a two-mile walk from the Dyer's home to the Boston-Charlestown ferry. As it was still snowing, the oxen had not yet started to clear the roads, and it was not possible for horses or carts to traverse. Mary prepared herself with all the wool she could assemble topped by a heavy hooded cape. As the Dyers pushed through the drifts on their way across Boston, the snow adhered to Mary's long skirt which became heavy as armour with the freezing of her hem. As they approached the ferry landing,[2] Mary and William were relieved to find their jolly friend, Thomas Marshall, waiting with his scow. He had his oars ready as there were too many ice flows to set sail. It was a half a mile's row through the fast falling snowflakes to Charlestown. As they approached the dock on Water Street, Mary could see a blurred crowd of observers waiting to watch them land. A tall ladder shiny with ice was the only access from the water to the dock. Mary's frozen little English boots started to slip as she mounted. Her fingers were so numb that she could hardly grasp the rungs through her stiff mittens.

The people on the dock directed the Dyers towards the Indian path which led about five miles through the woods from Charlestown to Newtowne. As it was compulsory to carry firearms through these woods, William had brought his gun. He also wore a padded jacket against any stray Indian arrows.[3]

After several hours of trudging through the snow, Mary and William arrived in Newtowne. There was a rustling of excitement among the gathering of people as they approached the Meeting House.[4]

The Dyers were followed by many searching eyes as they entered the Meeting House to take their seats. They sat on opposite sides in silent gloom waiting to hear the worst. It was hard for Mary to overhear the asides exchanged between the people watching them. The meeting finally came to order. With each announcement, their worst apprehensions turned into grim realities. John Wheelwright was the first to be convicted of "constructive sedition" and sentenced to disenfranchisement and exile. He was given fourteen days to leave Massachusetts. Two of the three deputies of the General Court had also been disenfranchised and exiled: William Aspinwall for being the author of the Boston petition, and John Coggeshall for his strong support.[5] John Coggeshall and William Aspinwall were Deacons of the First Church as well as deputies for Boston. They were both expelled from the General Court. As William Coddington was the only one of three deputies who had not signed the petition for Wheelwright, he alone was allowed to retain his seat as Treasurer of the colony. Governor Vane's former escorts, Edward Hutchinson and William Baulston, were both disenfranchised for their disrespect to Governor Winthrop when they threw down their halberds at the time of Harry Vane's defeat. They were also fined, and when Hutchinson refused to pay he was jailed for a few days. Governor Winthrop had his eye on four other men who were "as apt to meddle in public affairs beyond [their] calling and skill." They were Thomas Marshall, deacon and shoemaker as well as ferryman, William Dyneley, the barber, Richard Gridley, the brick-maker and fence overseer, and William Dyer, known as Mary Dyer's husband, and a signer of the petition. All of them were deprived of their right to vote and banished from the Colony. The majority of Boston inhabitants were for Vane, but the outlying towns voted for Winthrop. They did not have to leave immediately like Wheelwright. Because of the severe weather they were given until spring to make their plans. Where would they all go? Back to England?

Anne Hutchinson was summoned before the afternoon court for "traducing the ministers and their ministry in the colony." She arrived just in time to hear the morning decisions before bracing herself for her own trial. As she entered the Meeting House, the first person she saw was Mary Dyer. Their eyes locked for a moment of shared courage and resignation.

The magistrates were seated facing the people. They were Thomas Dudley, Roger Hardekdon, Increase Nowell, Israel Stoughton, Richard Bellingham, John Hunfry, Jennison John Endicott, William Coddington, and William Colburn. The ministers were all in black, with forked Geneva neckbands, stiff and glossy with starch. They were Zachariah Symnes of Charlestown, George Phillips of Watertown, Thomas Shepherd of Newtowne, John Wilson and John Cotton from Boston, Thomas Weld and John Eliot from Roxbury, and Hugh Peters from Salem. Simon Bradstreet, the Court's scribe, was warming his ink pot over a charcoal brazier.

Governor Winthrop arrived, escorted by his honor guard. He was both judge and prosecutor at this trial. He took his seat in the middle of the magistrates and opened the meeting by saying, "Mrs. Hutchinson, you have troubled the peace of the Commonwealth and the churches here. You have uttered many things against our churches and ministers and continued to hold meetings in your house that are considered condemned as a thing not tolerable in the sight of God nor fitting for your sex. Therefore, we have brought you here that you may plainly see your error and repent; but if you do not, the Court will see that you trouble us no longer."[7]

Anne Hutchinson's trial went on for two days. Governor Winthrop's accusations focused on the fact that she, a woman, had no right to be heard.[8] He demanded to be shown anything in the scripture which gave her the right to teach either women or men. Anne was quick to respond, "Priscilla with her husband instructed Apollos.[9] Phebe was a deaconess in the early Church. Deborah was a judge!" Mary Dyer was smiling at Anne's deft replies. Anne knew at least as much as the magistrates.

Governor Winthrop pursued his objection to the meetings held at Anne's house. "You have seduced honest people from their work and families. All the present troubles have arisen from those who attend your meetings. We see no rule of God for this. If you will not stop these meetings, we will have to restrain you."[10] He asked her why she held meetings every week on a set day. Anne's response was, "It is just as lawful for me to do so as any of the rulers or ministers. Is there one standard for men and another for women?" She went on to explain that she considered the value of her meetings as giving an excellent opportunity for her sex to ask the questions which would otherwise go unasked.

Anne was becoming very weary towards the end of the second day of the inquisition. She said, "Now if you do condemn me for speaking what in my conscience I know to be the truth, I must commit myself unto the Lord ... Take heed how you proceed against me."

Anne then told of the revelations she had had in England. It was a bad mistake. Anne's quick wit and knowledge of the Bible had served to keep her on top of the situation until this moment. Revelations were an unforgivable sin. The Puritans believed God's word was only to be found in the Scripture and never by direct communication.

For Governor Winthrop, her move was decisive: "The Court is convinced that Mrs. Hutchinson's views are both erroneous and dangerous. We cannot permit her to continue preaching them. Therefore, if you agree that she ought to be imprisoned until such a time as she can be banished from the colony, hold up your right hand."

All but three of the Magistrates raised their right hands. Deputy Jennison was undecided, William Colburn disagreed, William Coddington not only disagreed, but accused Governor Winthrop of acting illegally as both judge and prosecutor at the same time.

William Dyer and William Hutchinson, along with fifty-six other citizens from Boston and seventeen others from nearby towns, were eventually either banished or disenfranchised. All seventy-five heads of these families were ordered to leave their "guns, pistols, swords, powder, shot and match" at Mr. Keayne's tavern by November 30, upon "pain of ten pounds for every default" and not to receive them back again until they acknowledged their sin in subscribing to sedition.[11] It was clear that he feared a revolution — but, not so clear how the banished families were expected to survive in the wilderness without any means of protection.

Governor Winthrop still felt that Massachusetts Bay Colony was like a private estate which he was justified in controlling. He decided that exclusion was the best way of dealing with deviance, and drafted laws requiring the magistrates' approval of any newcomer entering the colony, hoping to halt the arrival of more Hutchinson relatives from England.

Anne was sent to spend the winter in Roxbury before banishment in March. "Rocksborough" center was an outcrop of conglomerate rocks which stood over a narrow landing in Boston. She was under house arrest, staying with the family of Joseph Weld, brother of Thomas Weld. There she remained for four months, removed from her family and friends who "might be contaminated by her doctrines." However, she was besieged with visits all winter by the ministers she had most provoked by her heresies. Thomas Weld, living across the street, came most often. He was usually accompanied by Thomas Shepherd from Newtowne and John Eliot. They heckled her with challenges. Anne rose to every debate. The ministers could not get her to admit any errors. In despair, they made a collection of the "growing evils of her secret opinions."

Winthrop described that winter in his journal: "Killing ice and snowstorms, packed in high winds so that the only reason anyone went outside for days on end was to cut wood for warmth near the fire and cooking."

But Mary Dyer could not be kept away. Whenever possible, she would sneak across the windswept icy two-mile strip of land that separated Roxbury from Boston. As she was not allowed to visit with Anne, their meetings often consisted of frosty whispers through the crack of a window.

For Anne Hutchinson and Mary Dyer, their world had become ceilinged with icicles, any one of which could fall unexpectedly upon them. They could not see what the future held; it was like the unseen seven-eighths of an iceberg.

{ 8 }
Cast Out of the Church

When Anne returned to Boston from house arrest in Roxbury in March, most of her supporters had left to look for a new place to live, including her husband William Hutchinson and William Dyer. With these dissidents out of the way, it seemed like a good time for a church trial. The magistrates were not satisfied that Anne had suffered the excommunication she deserved. As she had not been allowed to sign the Wheelwright petition, she could not be marked for banishment with the others who had. Since she was not a "free woman," they could not take that away from her. However, as a member of the Boston Church, they could call her "to account in a church way."

The Congregational Church believed that each church was founded on its own covenant and that anyone violating that covenant was subject to censure by the Church. No discipline could be imposed without the consent of the members of the Church. It was up to the congregation to determine whether Anne Hutchinson deserved the extreme punishment of being cast out of the Church.

Anne's church trial was called for 10:00 a.m. on March 22, 1638.[1] Much to the annoyance of the assembled clergy, she came in late. This time, John Wilson and John Cotton represented the ecclesiastics as the inquisitors, with Governor John Winthrop and Deputy Governor Thomas Dudley also present. Anne's son Edward and her son-in-law, Thomas Savage, were the only supporters left on the men's side of the Church. Mary Dyer sat in the pew behind Anne Hutchinson on the women's side. For the first time, the church members were separated from the non-members and asked to sit in the front of the church, so that the voters could be distinguished from those not eligible to express their opinion. Anne was asked to stand while all others sat. Her pregnancy was noticeable as she stood before the congregation. Mary Dyer watched her with concern as she stood for hours of unrelieved questioning. Several times she started to sway, as if she might faint. Finally, she was offered a stool to sit on.

John Wilson opened the meeting, and John Cotton asked to have read the twenty-nine alleged errors which had been collected by the ministers who had visited her during her house arrest in Roxbury — Thomas Weld, John Eliot, and Thomas Shepherd.

"What rule in the Holy Writ makes it right for elders of the church to question one in my confinement, pretending they sought light, but seeking to entrap me in my own words?" Anne had trusted the Church to support her. She could hardly believe that the Boston congregation could pack the Church with a spirit of curiosity rather than compassion.

Each minister had his own insult to express. Thomas Shepherd of Cambridge called Anne "a very dangerous woman to sow her corrupt opinion to the infection of many."

Hugh Peters said, "You have stepped out of your place; you have rather been a husband than a wife; and a preacher than a hearer; and a magistrate than a subject."

Wilson added his opinion: "I look at her as a dangerous instrument of the devil."

Exhausted, Anne was reduced to meekness. She said, "I spoke rashly and unadvisedly. I do not allow the slighting of ministers, nor of the Scriptures, nor anything that is set up by God. It was never in my heart to slight any man, but only that man should be kept in his own place and not set in the room of God."

It was Cotton's betrayal that hurt Anne the most. He accused her of lying. It was hard to believe that the man she had followed across the Atlantic had turned away from her.

John Wilson also accused Anne of speaking falsely and ambiguously. His final statement was: "I do cast you out — I do deliver you up to Satan — I do account you from this time forth to be a heathen — I command you in the name of Christ Jesus and of the Church as a leper to withdraw your self." The finality of Wilson's statement was underlined when the ministers rose to turn their backs on her. The congregation was denied their right to vote and it became obvious to Anne that the trial was over and she had been excommunicated.[2]

Anne got up from her stool and started to walk out of the church. Mary Dyer quickly rose to follow her. Hand in hand they walked out of the hushed church. There was not a sound until they reached the steps of the church. Anne hesitated on the top step and threw back her head to exclaim, "The Lord judgeth not as man judgeth. Better to be cast out of the church than to deny Christ."

As the two women descended the church steps hand in hand, there were several women hanging around outside the church and one was heard to ask, "Who is that woman accompanying Anne Hutchinson?"

Another voice answered loud enough to be heard inside the church, "She is the mother of a monster!"

This last audible sentence obliterated and superseded all that Governor Winthrop had heard in the church trial. Excited and frantically curious, he questioned Cotton about "the mother of a monster." Cotton broke down and confessed that "God, Cotton and Anne Hutchinson" had buried a deformed child five months ago. Governor Winthrop insisted that he be shown the place of burial. Although the child had been buried "too deep for dog or hog," it was not too deep for Winthrop. He ordered the child exhumed and brought to him for examination. In a frenzy of excitement, he observed the spoils of misfortune. Having heard that Goody Hawkins was present at the delivery, he sent for her to give him a description of the child at birth. Goody Hawkins arrived brimming over with lurid descriptions of the "face without a head, the horns, the two mouths, and claws for feet." Governor Winthrop took careful notes on the abnormalities, never questioning the veracity of Goody Hawkins, who was soon to be banished from Massachusetts for being a "witch."[3]

Winthrop would publicize his description of the unfortunate birth for all the world to confirm that he was right and therefore justified in banishing someone so inspired by the devil as Mary Dyer.[4] As the Dyers and Hutchinsons prepared for their departure, Winthrop composed letters to Thomas Hooker in Connecticut, Governor Bradford in Plymouth, Roger Williams in Providence, Roger Brims and Sir Symond D'Eves in London as well as other notables around the world describing with gory skill the deformities of the tiny dead girl. The recipients of this letter responded sympathetically to Winthrop. Roger Williams' supportive remarks were that "God has a way of responding to his people." "I also humbly thank you for that sad relation of the monster, etc. The Lord speaks once and twice: he be pleased to open all our ears to his disciplines."[5]

In the meantime John Cotton was called before the congregation of his church to repent for having assisted in the secret burial of Mary's child.

Mary Dyer's life had been turned inside out for all the world to observe. No privacy was left when John Cotton was driven to apologize before the entire Boston congregation for befriending her in her hour of need. The image of this God-loving woman had been blackened by a powerful cluster of men who now chose to stigmatize her as mistress to the devil. Mary wept afresh for all those kidnapped from God's universal community, excluded from membership in the Boston Church. She knew that her experience could be crushing and destructive of her aspirations. She must turn inward for strength and look upwards for light. Her religious quest in an unkind world was not just for herself; eventually it would be extended to all the religious homeless. But this would take time.

{ 9 }
The "Bodie Politick"
and the Portsmouth Compact

W hile Boston was in the midst of the Antinomian Trials, another impressive young man slipped into their midst. John Clarke arrived in November, 1637. He was born in Westhorpe, England, in 1609 and had migrated to Holland where he was educated at the University of Leyden. He was distinguished for his scholarship in ancient languages, law, medicine, and theology. In fellowship with many Baptists in Holland, he picked up a strong taste for religious freedom. He came to Boston with high expectations for the New World. Astounded to find the whole colony trapped by disagreement on salvation and seemingly oblivious to the possibilities of the wilderness that surrounded them, he wrote his first impressions:

> I was no sooner on shore, but there appeared to me differences among them touching the covenants ... I thought it not strange to see men differ about matters of Heaven, for I expect no less on earth; but to see that they were not able so to bear each other in their different understandings and consciences as in the utmost part of the world live peaceably together ... for as much as the land was before us and wide enough — to turn aside to the right hand or to the left ...[1]

John Clarke attended the trials of John Wheelwright and Anne Hutchinson and became immediately sympathetic with the Antinomians. After Wheelwright was banished, John Clarke volunteered to help him seek out another place to live. They headed north to Exeter,

New Hampshire, with eight others. There he founded a colony where he practiced medicine for one winter. Clarke described his first exploration: "I went north to be somewhat cooler, but the winter following proved so cold that we were forced in the spring to make towards the south."[2] He parted with Wheelwright after this unsuccessful venture. It was fortunate for the Dyers and their friends that John Clarke minded the cold. They were in need of a young leader to help them find a new place and a new way of pursuing their ideals.

When John Clarke returned to Boston in early March, he consulted with the banished Antinomians and they agreed to meet on March 7, 1638. Eighteen men gathered quietly at the only brick house in Boston, the home of William Coddington. They were: William Aspinwall, William Baulston, Henry Bull, Richard Carder, John Coggeshall, William Coddington, William Dyer, William Freeborne, Randall Holden, Edward Hutchinson, Edward Hutchinson, Jr., William Hutchinson, John Porter, John Sanford, Thomas Savage, Philip Shearman, John Walker and Samuel Wilbore. The occasion was both serious and creative. With tallow candles flickering, they crowded around an oaken table to give form to their greatest aspirations. Although William Coddington was their natural leader, it was the newest and youngest, John Clarke, who found the words to express what they were trying to do. Their initial step was the organization of a regular government. They incorporated themselves into a "Bodie Politick, to submit [their] persons, lives, estates unto Lord Jesus, King of Lords, and to all those and absolute laws of his given in His Holy Word of Truth guided and judged thereby." It was John Clarke who composed the Portsmouth Compact, the object of which was "to lay the foundation of a Christian state where all who bore the name might worship God according to dictates of conscience untrammelled by written articles of faith and unawed by civil power."[3]

With solemnity and sincerity, these men shook hands on their agreement to do what they felt needed to be done. In the urgency of the moment, they did not realize the uniqueness of their compact. It was to be the first self-selected democratic group in the world organized by freemen independent of church or colonial obligation. It was to combine self-government with civil and religious freedom, obedience in law and full submission to their leader. William Coddington was selected as judge, for which he was accorded the greatest respect and "all due honor [unto him] according to the Lawes of God." And William Dyer was elected clerk.

After this famous gathering at William Coddington's brick house, an expedition was organized to search for a new place where the "Bodie Politick" could move with their families and put into action the ideals agreed upon in the Portsmouth Compact.

They were still without firearms. Although thirty-five of the seventy-five men who were ordered disarmed had recanted, Coddington's group remained stalwart, protesting loudly. But when they saw no remedy, they finally, reluctantly, obeyed and recanted in order to retrieve their one source of protection.

John Clarke assured the Bodie Politick that the chilly north was out of the question. Think south. Roger Williams came immediately to mind. He had been settled in Providence for two years and he would be just the person to advise. William Coddington summoned Captain William Cooley and his vessel to sail on an exploration to the south. Among those who boarded his ship in Boston harbor were John Clarke, William Dyer, William Hutchinson, Randall Holden, John Sanford, John Porter, and Richard Carder. They sailed as far as Cape Cod and then disembarked while Captain Cooley took his ship "about the large and dangerous cape."

After several days of exploring the woods, following Indian trails and fording streams, the seven weary men arrived at the home of Roger Williams. It was built on a point of land with an expansive view of Narragansett Bay to the south. Sheltering forests stretched to the northeast and fields to the southwest awaited cultivation. It was an ideal location. Roger Williams greeted the seven wanderers warmly. Mary Williams and their two little daughters had recently arrived from Salem, and she was quick with her own welcome of roast turkey and warm space by the fireplace. The members of the Bodie Politick were eager to learn anything they could from Roger Williams about creating a colony and the availability of land. They filled their beer mugs and lit their pipes for an evening of exchange. Bonded by banishment from the Massachusetts Bay Colony, Roger was ready to share his experience.

As conversation continued well into the night, it became obvious that Roger Williams had not set out to found a colony. Instead the colony had found Roger. There were twelve families, most of whom were freed servants who had followed him from Salem and Plymouth. He had divided the land equally with six acres for each family. Bound to one another only by brotherly love, they had no boundary lines, no patent, no deed, no regular government and no governor. Roger was not officially the head of anything, but he had the most influence. John Clarke and William Coddington found Roger Williams in need of administrative skills. His followers were largely farmers without educational opportunities, in contrast to the number of Cambridge graduates in their group. Clarke and Coddington became even more convinced that very careful planning would be essential to creating the colony they had in mind.

Roger's greatest contribution was his knowledge of the Narragansett Indians. It had been his dearest desire to be an apostle to the Indians and he had paddled up and down Narragansett Bay visiting them "in their stinking holes" and learning their language and customs. As Roger had become very knowledgeable about the surrounding land, John Clarke asked him where the banished Antinomians might resettle. Roger advised that the two best locations were Souwamas and the island of Aquidneck. He counseled Clarke to go to Plymouth to see whether either of these desired locations were claimed by another patent, and volunteered to accompany them there.

After a night of warm hospitality, Roger introduced his guests to the local method of preparing food for traveling, which he had learnt from the Wompanaug Indians the winter of his escape through the wintry woods from Salem to Providence, when he hardly knew "what bread or bed did mean." Uncovering the leaves over a pit in the ground, he unearthed some of the dried kernels of corn stored there. Always, while traveling, Roger carried a pouch of these dried kernels around his neck. When mashed and added to boiling water, in Indian fashion, they made delicious hominy " the very best traveling food. Each man helped himself to a pouchful before starting back through the woods to Plymouth.

Arriving in Plymouth, Roger Williams and the Bodie Politick contacted the Magistrates who, despite his differences with them, "lovingly gave [them] a meeting."[4] They were informed that "Souwamas" was the "flower in the garden" of the Plymouth Patent and not available to them. John Clarke reassured them that the newcomers would not settle there, and went on to inquire whether or not Plymouth also lay claim to the islands in Narragansett Bay, particularly Aquidneck. With "cheerful countenance" the magistrates recommended that they settle in Aquidneck, promising that Plymouth would "assist them as loving neighbours."

After this congenial meeting, John Clarke, relieved and elated, proclaimed "we're now on wing and resolved to clear!" On the way back to Providence, John Clarke consulted with Roger Williams about what they should do next. They decided to proceed to Aquidneck and confer with the local Sachem, Wonnumentonomey, about purchasing the island. He referred them to his overlords, Chief Sachems, Canonicus and Miantonomo, who lived in the town of Narragansett. Fortunately, Captain Cooley's ship had arrived in Providence in time to sail them across Narragansett Bay.

On March 27, 1638, they drew up a deed in which Canonicus and Miantonomo sold to Mr. Coddington and "the friends united with him" the great island of Aquidneck and also the marsh and grass upon Quinuiqut (Jamestown) and the rest of the islands of the bay except Chiachwessa (Prudence), sold already to Governor Winthrop and Roger Williams, and the grass upon the rivers and coves about Kittackquamuckquiet to Pumposquatick for the full payment of 40 fathoms of white "wompi" beads.[5] This "wampum" signified the Indian badge of wealth. The white "wompi" was made from the central part of the cockle shell of whelk or periwinkle and was half as valuable as the purple "sacki" which came from the shell of quahog pieces formed into tiny cylinders, polished smooth as stone. Beads of wampum were strung on thongs of deerskin and worn as necklaces and belts by the Indians.

Miantonomo was also to be given ten coats and twenty hoes to present to the inhabitants of Aquidneck so that they should remove themselves off the island the following winter, with the understanding that they could return for hunting and fishing. The deed was signed with the bow and arrow symbols of Canonicus and Miantonomo and the signatures of Roger Williams and Randall Holden. Wonnumentonomey, the Sachem of Aquidneck, received five fathoms of wampum and consented to the contents of the deed. Afterwards, Roger Williams summed up the sale when he declared, "It was not price nor money that could have purchased Rhode Island. Rhode Island was obtained by LOVE: the love and favour which that honorable gentleman, Harry Vane, and myself had with the great Sachem Miantonomo, about the league which I procured between the Massachusetts English and the Narragansetts in the Pequot War." Roger Williams knew well that his friends could never have purchased Aquidneck for forty fathoms of "wompi" without his acting as the benevolent real estate agent.

After the signing of the deed that purchased Aquidneck, John Clarke, William Dyer, William Coddington, Randall Holden, and others sailed joyfully back to Pocasset across Narragansett Bay. On March 24, 1638, they sailed close to Prudence Island which Roger Williams had bought the previous year for himself and Governor Winthrop. On the leeward side, a very small island peered up from the depths of Narragansett Bay. For William Dyer, it was love at first sight. He saw this little island absolutely centrifugal to the whole of Narragansett Bay, a perfect centerpiece to the large body of water. William Dyer begged to land and explore the island and Coddington granted his request. The sandy shore was lined with mussels and clams. Birds flew up from the marshy grasses and inland ponds. William Dyer knew that this island was included in the package purchased from the Indians. The deed had been signed to include the outlying islands. In a moment of unabashed exaltation, he declared to Coddington, "This is the island of my eye. It is my heart's greatest desire to possess it. I want it for my very own." Coddington was glad to grant a favor to the man who had been such a helpful assistant to him as secretary, and responded, "It is not so much the value of the land, but for William Dyer's love of it and asking for it that I grant it to him."[6]

All the men on board stood as witnesses to the gift of this island of six hundred acres to William Dyer.[7] They could not help but tease him for falling in love with an island. As Roger Williams later wrote, reaffirming Dyer's right to the island, "Sometimes in merriment, but always in earnest [the island] granted to be not only in name but in truth and reality the Proper Right; and Inheritance of Mr. William Dyer."

After leaving Narragansett Bay the "Bodie Politick" sailed around the Cape to return to their families who were eagerly awaiting the news of where they were going to live next. Back in Boston within a week, William Dyer walked with a bounding step from the docks to Summer Street. He was brimming with good tidings as he entered his home. Contrary to his expectations, he found a very dejected Mary, which tempered his elation. He soon discovered what had befallen her, a sharp contrast to his happy adventure. Two days after he had received his island gift and was sailing merrily home, his Mary, hand-in-hand with Anne Hutchinson, was ejected from the Boston Church. William was not accustomed to seeing Mary in tears, and he had to decipher what she was saying between the sobs. William finally learned that Governor Winthrop had pronounced Mary the "mother of a monster," and had ordered their infant to be dug up so that he could observe the abnormalities himself and report them to the whole wide world to justify the banishment of the Antinomians.

The Antinomians were told that, if they did not leave before May, they would have to appear in the General Court again. Without much time for preparations, all of the families of the "Bodie Politick" hustled to get ready for the departure. They had houses and land to sell. William Dyer sold his home, his share of the town pier, and his fields on Rommeys Marsh and Pullens Point, while William Brenton and William Coddington held onto some of their land in Massachusetts Bay Colony. Everyone had livestock as well as household possessions to transport. Some went by land and some by sea.

The Coddingtons left by sea on April 26. The Dyers accompanied the Hutchinsons by land, stopping at Mount Wollaston before going on to Providence. They followed an Indian trail, single file, around

Mount Hope. There, they awaited the arrival of many of their possessions sent by ship. As they paused on the shore, Mary could just make out the outline of the island which was to be her future home across the bay.

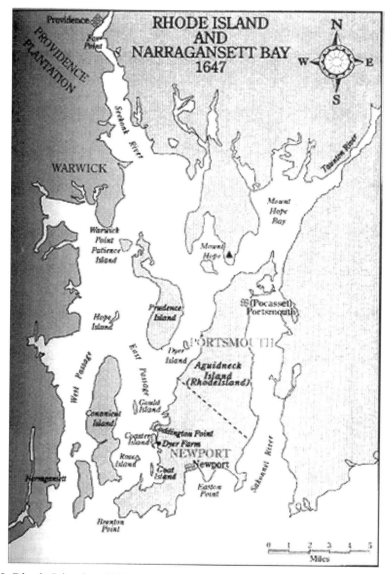

9. Rhode Island and Narragansett Bay 1647(drawn by Philip Schwartzberg)

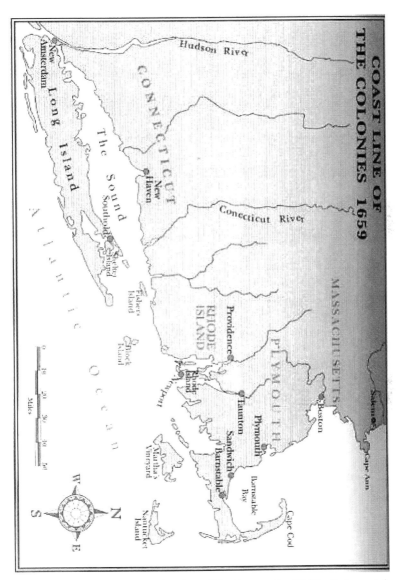

10. Coastline of the Colonies in 1659 (drawn by Philip Schwartzb-erg).

{ 10 }
"Wonders" in Pocasset*

When Mary Dyer stepped onto the shores of the northern-most tip of Aquidneck, she must have felt as if civilization was retrogressing. Pocasset was so much more primitive than those first days in Boston, where the bare bones of a community were already established and the homes of earlier settlers stood available for newcomers. Pocasset represented the un-tampered wilderness. The banished Antinomians were the first of the English to settle there. Survival depended on total self-sufficiency, as the motherland became ever more remote. On the shores of Boston, one could scan the horizon with hopes that any white speck might grow into the sail of a bark or brig coming from England with more people, news, and supplies. Here, those distant light patches remained seagulls or whitecaps, for no transatlantic ship then set its course towards the Pocasset cove.

Shelter was the primary concern. A few people crawled into the caves which they discovered along the banks of the cove where they landed. Mary and William Dyer chose to imitate the Indians they had observed bending birches into house frames, slapping mud into instant walls, and weaving twigs to make thatched roofs. A cluster of such mud shelters sprang up like mushrooms overnight. They would have to serve as temporary quarters until the Antinomians had time to consider a more permanent design for the community.

The first nights in the little mud huts were orchestrated by the sustained howls of wolves, accompanied by the staccato sobs of Samuel Dyer and the other terrified children. In Boston, the night calls of the wolves had sounded like distant echoes in the faraway woods, separated as they were from the mainland by Rocksborough

Neck.
* Later renamed Portsmouth

In Pocasset, the plaintive calls increased in volume as the wolves sniffed out the unprotected settlement by the cove.

An even more serious consideration for the anxious people snuggled together in their makeshift shelters was the unprotected livestock. The Dyers had transported their horses, cows, sheep and hogs. The animals lay limp with exhaustion after their rough sea voyage around Cape Cod, vulnerable to the night prowling of the hungry wolves. It was obvious that something would have to be done about the wolf menace — immediately.

William Coddington called a special meeting of all the men to discuss what they should do. William Dyer, John Coggeshall, William Hutchinson, John Clarke, William Brenton, and all the others, walked over to the little mud hut built by the spring to serve as a Meeting House. Mary waited in anticipation to hear the men's decision. With her husband as secretary for the "Bodie Politick" she had easy access to the latest news. William felt proud to have Mary read his notes.[1]

Although there were many amateur suggestions as to how to handle wolves, no one felt confident. Finally, the puzzled men of the "Bodie Politick" decided to consult Roger Williams, who had several more years of experience, and a host of Indian friends familiar with the ways of the wilds. Roger Williams was at his home in Providence when he received the call for help. Within twenty-four hours he appeared off Pocasset with two hundred Narragansett Indians in a fleet of canoes.

Mary had never encountered so many Indians at one time. She had met the Narragansett Sachem, Miantonomo, in Boston the preceding year when he came to meet with Governor Harry Vane. There had been a feast for the visiting Indians and rockets flared from the ships in Boston Harbor to celebrate the signing of a treaty between the Puritans and the Narragansett Indians against the warlike Pequot Indians. John Winthrop and the other Boston magistrates thought the celebration was excessive and contrary to Puritan tradition, but when exuberant Harry Vane threw his arms around the surprised Miantonomo, it seemed like the first real embrace between England and native America.

The Narragansetts beached their canoes on the shore. The canoes were shaped like tree-trunks, hollowed out by burning and scraping, made large enough to hold 30-40 men. The prevailing wind carried a strong smell of raccoon fat, used by the Indians to grease their bodies. Loin cloths of deerskin were their only clothing, but their arms and legs were decorated with wampum bracelets and some had bone pendants or beads to complete their costuming. These were the same Indians who formerly lived on the Pocasset Point and evacuated to Connanicutt (Jamestown) to accommodate the "white man." Roger Williams had learned their languages, studied their customs, and paddled miles to visit them in their homes. As a result, they had left "out of love for Roger Williams" and now they were returning "out of love for Roger Williams." The Narragansett Indians would do almost anything for Roger. This time, he persuaded them to conduct a wolf drive on Pocasset Point.

Mary watched the Indians dig a deep pit by the sea. With crude shovels they worked in unison, swiftly tossing the sandy soil to one side. Once satisfied with the depth of the pit, they disappeared into the woods, soon to return with a wounded deer, which they placed as a lure on the bottom of the pit. Then, with whoops and hollers and flying arrows, they rounded up a pack of wolves and stampeded them towards the trap. As the singing woods turned into a screaming jungle, Mary clapped her hands over her ears to dull the shrieks. It was not for long. The pit became a wolf grave and there were twenty fewer wolves to prowl around the English settlers at night. Mary overheard Roger Williams remind William Coddington that the Indian Chief, Miantonomo, might like a present for his services — like sugar.

Coddington realized that more permanent protection from the wolves would also be necessary.[2] Fences were essential. The "Bodie Politick" gathered again at the Meeting House to discuss fence specifications. It was decided that five rails with no more than three inches between each rail would prove an adequate design for excluding wolves. The first fence was built around a common pasture for the whole town.

Next in importance was the allotment of land for more permanent housing. John Clarke was chosen to survey the land and William Dyer was selected to assign six acre lots to each man, with the understanding that each property owner must build a house within a year, and pay the treasurer, William Hutchinson, two shillings for every acre of land. William Dyer was responsible for drawing up the property deeds and holding them in safekeeping as proof of individual ownership, which left him in a position of considerable power.

As the woods chimed with the sinking of axes and the wilderness was transformed with the delineations of the English, the "Bodie Politick" became aware that these rising fences could only give partial protection. Men must be ready with more aggressive action, if necessary. Edward Hutchinson and William Baulston (the spirited guards who had assisted Henry Vane during his governorship), were chosen as training sergeants. It was decided that every man between the age of 18 and 50 years should drill for regular service. Each man would be allotted "one muskett, one pound of powder, twenty bulletts, two fademe of matches, with sword, and bandeliers all completely furnished." It was compulsory to bear arms. Anyone found two miles from town unarmed or, attending a meeting without arms, would be fined. More elaborate plans were made to meet emergencies. An alarm system was devised by which drums would be steadily beaten while a messenger ran from house to house alerting the inhabitants of any impending danger.

William Baulston had more to do than train the troops. As the former Boston innkeeper, he was soon licensed to "set up a house of entertainment for strangers and also to brew beare and to sell wines of strong waters and such necessary provisions as may be useful in any kind." As the British were not accustomed to drinking water, beer was considered a dire necessity, but drunkenness was punishable. Henry Bull was assigned sergeant to attend all meetings of the judge and elders and "to inform of all breaches of the Lawes of God that tend to civil disturbances," and a jail was built adjoining his house with stocks and a whipping post placed nearby.

In all matters, the interests of the individual were regarded as secondary to the welfare of the group. In this respect, the "Bodie Politick" differed dramatically from the settlement at Providence Plantation. Roger Williams tended to place the wishes of the individual ahead of the concerns of the group. This resulted in very different growth patterns between the mainland and the island of the emerging colony. While Providence was experiencing a casual evolution, the "Bodie Politick" was busy trying to anticipate any emergency.

Despite their careful consideration of all possible crises, the "Bodie Politick" was utterly unprepared for the earthquake of August 1638.[3] No one would ever forget what he or she was doing when it happened. At that dreadful moment, there was no way of knowing that it was a coastwide happening and not just a local experience. For two minutes, the earth shook violently. Everyone was jarred from position, no matter what they were doing. While William Coddington was working on the mast of his pinnace, the calmness of the Pocasset cove suddenly churned choppier than the English Channel. Startled and unprepared, Coddington was tossed from the top of his mast and plunged into the water below. Brenton reported that he saw monsters among his sheep.

It took weeks of stillness for the people to re-establish a trust in the ground upon which they walked. The most reassuring news was the report that Boston had also had its shaking. Aquidneck had not been singled out for this disaster. The fields of Connecticut were reported to be under ten feet of water, and the people were starving. It was a universal happening. The "Bodie Politick" had not been selected for punishment.

The inhabitants of Pocasset were just beginning to take a firm foothold for granted again when nature produced another unexpected phenomenon. It was a surprisingly chilly day for August, and the clouds were assembling like black puff balls over Pocasset. Large fluffy snowflakes whirled and spun for seconds before they fell and melted on the ground. The inhabitants did not take this seasonal confusion as seriously as the more threatening earthquake, but they did wonder what God was trying to tell them by releasing snowflakes in August. It was one more cause for uneasiness.

During this time of environmental aberrations, Anne Hutchinson, expecting her fourteenth child, experienced a menopausal mishap which, like Mary Dyer's obstetrical disaster of 1637, was reported as a "monster birth." It did not take long for the rumors to reach Boston. Governor Winthrop was heartened by the evidence that the Antinomians were still being "punished" for challenging the Puritan stronghold. He was too far away to make another personal inspection of the "monster" as he had done in the case of Mary Dyer. Learning that John Clarke had attended Anne Hutchinson as her physician, John Winthrop demanded a report.[4] Although it seems out of character for Dr. Clarke to respond to such a request, he answered Governor Winthrop's demand with lurid details, thereby supplying the Boston ministers and magistrates with one more weapon in their battle against the Antinomians.

In the 17th century unexpected, unexplainable events, such as a monster birth, storm, devastating fire, earthquake, rainbow, or an eclipse, were called "Wonders." Such wonders evidenced the will of God and they were interpreted as God's punishment to errant man.[5] There were no scientific explanations for these natural aberrations. The church forbade both men and women to ask questions.

Although the Pocasset settlers left Boston not planning to return, the remaining Puritans had second thoughts about letting some of their distinguished citizens go. Scouts were sent to some of the outlying towns to retrieve many of the outcast and restore to them all of their former privileges. John Cotton, who already had a reputation for see-sawing his allegiances, sent some deputies from the Boston Church to journey to Pocasset to try and reclaim some of the members who had left without any ecclesiastical censure. Anne Hutchinson was the only person who had actually been excommunicated. Cotton made a special appeal to the Coggeshalls, Coddingtons, and Dyers to remain members of the Boston Church. William Dyer had no desire for reconciliation. He did not see what business the Boston Church had in interfering with the affairs of Aquidneck. William Coddington and John Coggeshall agreed with

Dyer. It is not known why, but of them all, only Mary expressed a desire to remain a member. She stood alone in her disappointment when John Cotton told the Boston Church that if the Dyers, Coddingtons and Coggeshalls remained "obstinate" a law would be passed to expel them from Massachusetts. It would seem as if this had been taken care of the preceding year, but there was obvious conflict over the finality.

It was during this period that Pocasset received a visitor who breezed in like a veritable cyclone. Samuel Gorton had just come from Plymouth which had thrown him out. Wherever he went, Samuel Gorton was quick to insert his rebellious spirit in the crucial areas of dissatisfaction. Anne Hutchinson had a weakness for high-spirited people and she gave him the opportunity he was seeking.

Anne Hutchinson had thrived on her experience in Boston where most of the town gathered in her house in a search for the real meaning of life. Mary Dyer had joyfully shared this new-found opportunity for women to express themselves. There was something very clarifying about the exchange of ideas. She had never felt so certain about her own convictions. When the Antinomians moved to Pocasset, Anne Hutchinson lost some of her spit and fire. Anne, with Mary at her side, had inspired the men to rise up and express their differences with the Puritan magistrates and ministers. Once these men had tasted their freedom, they reverted to a male world. Banished from Boston, they made all the decisions in Pocasset. No women were invited into the little mud Meeting House except to attend Church. As the presiding minister, John Clarke's sermons were too sensible to criticize and too down to earth to excite. Anne Hutchinson became more and more dissatisfied with her subsidiary role.

Samuel Gorton had a special appeal for Anne Hutchinson and Mary Dyer for he believed that anyone should be allowed to speak up in Church. Women were equal to men! They should be allowed to speak their minds, and what's more, they should be listened to. He wasted no time in exploring the dissatisfactions of Anne Hutchinson and conspiring with her on a plan which would change everything, suggesting that her one chance to express herself in the growth of the young community would be through her meek and mild, obedient and loving husband. If William Hutchinson could only replace William Coddington as Judge, Anne would have real influence.

Coddington was quite unaware of this intrigue when he left Aquidneck for a few days in Boston to tend to some business. Returning to Pocasset, he discovered to his utter amazement that William Hutchinson had replaced him as judge in a coup d'etat. He felt in his heart that this must be the dirty work of the despicable Samuel Gorton, who dared to question the right of the "Bodie Politick" to exist without a royal charter from King Charles I.

William Coddington was not cut out for second place, and his supporters began to feel a rift in the community. John Clarke and William Dyer had already done a lot of surveying to the south of the island, returning with maps of promising country. Coddington had a commercial eye for landscape. The possibilities of spacious areas of farming were described, but most important was the report of a large protected harbor, facing south, with far greater possibilities for trade than the Pocasset Cove. The community was beginning to divide between the supporters of William Hutchinson and William Coddington, who took a count of his potential followers and counted eighteen families ready to leave Pocasset and explore the southern tip of Aquidneck. He assigned Nicholas Easton and his two young sons, Peter and John, to explore the coast more carefully and designate the best place to land.

When Nicholas Easton returned to Pocasset, the Dyers slipped over to the Coddingtons to be among the first to hear about the expedition. Nicholas Easton, bursting with his report, described how he and his sons had started coasting in a canoe peacefully down the shoreline of Aquidneck.[6] By late afternoon, they came upon a lovely island. Peter and John wanted to land and explore and decided to spend the night there. Inspired by their relaxed style of traveling, they named the island, "Coaster." The next day they left Coaster's Island and paddled down the shores of Aquidneck until they discovered an exquisite harbor lying between the embracing arms of two points of land. The water was so deep that any pinnace could sail right up to the banks and moor to a tree. Leaving the perfect harbor, they paddled strenuously around a rocky point where they had to stiffen themselves against the prevailing surf. On the other side of this point they were rewarded with a vision of white sand gleaming in the midday sun. It was easy to wade ashore and pull their canoe up on the glorious beach. Feeling possessive as explorers, they called their find, "Easton's Beach." Although they did not like leaving the beach, the harbor or the island, they were eager to return and report to Coddington.

Nicholas Easton's report was like music to the ears of William Coddington. The time was ripe for departure from Pocasset. The month of May was a good one for moving. The destination was decided. Coddington would alert his followers.

Before leaving, William Coddington called William Dyer to his hut for a very private conversation. He reassured Dyer that the place they were leaving would soon be secondary to the place they were going. However, he did have some concerns in separating from the Hutchinson group. They had already been chided by members of the Massachusetts Bay Colony for "inventing a settlement" without the authority of Royal Patent. The most authentic claim they had to the land was the deed signed by Miantonomo. It was kept by William Dyer. Also in Dyer's custody were all the agreements made by the "Bodie Politick," and the deeds for individual grants of land in Pocasset. Final authority rested in these documents. When Coddington asked Dyer if he could manage to conceal them among his personal possessions when they left, Dyer agreed not to tell anyone, and to depart quickly before anything was discovered missing.

Coddington suggested that the Dyer family sail with the Coddingtons on their pinnace as soon as possible. The two men shook hands with the heartiness that seals a plot. Dyer then left to organize his departure.

William confided in Mary how important it was to keep the deeds both safe and secret. Not one other person must know of their plan to run off with them. Mary was accustomed to sharing plans with Anne Hutchinson. It was very hard to think that anything but honesty could pass between Mary Dyer and Anne Hutchinson. Mary felt her heart was about to crack with the idea of this departure and the unshared secret made it all the more difficult.

William Coddington alerted his followers to make ready with their families. They were Henry Bull, William Brenton, Jeremy Clarke, John Clarke, Joseph Clarke, Tom Clarke, John Coggeshall, William Coulie, William Dyer, Nicholas Easton, Robert Field, William Foster, George Gardner, Thomas Hazard, Robert Jeoffries, Robert Stanton and Samuel Wilbore. Along with the families were horses, goats, sheep, cattle, and hogs. Transportation would not be as difficult as the trip from Massachusetts Bay Colony, when they rounded Cape Cod in a storm. This time, it would be possible to bring the majority overland.

For the third time Mary and William Dyer gathered together all their worldly possessions to journey forth to an unknown territory and begin life in the colonies all over again. They hastened to make ready to sail on the Coddingtons' Pinnace. There were many awkward farewells. Mary tried to hold back the floodgates of her emotions when she parted with Anne. William's greatest consideration was the property deeds strapped inconspicuously between his shoulders.

11. Pinnace by John F. Leavitt (courtesy of the Peabody and Essex Museum, Salem, MA). The pinnace, with its deck, was most commonly used for transportation in Narragansett Bay.

12. Shallop by John F. Leavitt (courtesy of the Peabody and Essex Museum, Salem, MA). Shallops had no decks and were equipped with oars for rowing, handy for fishing. These boats were often constructed from the remains of shipwrecks.

{ 11 }
To Newport

The trip by sea was a new experience. The islands added a special interest to the sail down Narragansett Bay. Their different shapes and sizes decorated the passage of water and lent a sense of intimacy to sailing never experienced on the unbroken waterline of the vast Atlantic. William was eager for Mary to see "the island of his eye." Mary could hardly believe that this jewel in the watery wilderness already bore their name. As they tacked around Dyer Island, geese flew up from the inner marsh and honked their territorial prerogatives.

Sailing on close to the Aquidneck coastline felt like invading a primeval forest. "The island was well wooded and watered with good soil and diversity of hill and dale pleasing to the eye."[1] When Coddington saw water to the southeast, he knew they were reaching the tip of the island which was their destination. The depth and breadth of the harbor made for an easy access. They sailed right up to the bank without touching bottom. Coddington selected a sturdy elm leaning over the water to hitch up his pinnace. The other families from Pocasset arrived in installments with their livestock, some by land and some by sea. Once more, they started living in caves and the crudest huts as their temporary shelters while they considered their future.

On May 19, 1639, they gathered for the first town meeting in the new locale, to elect William Coddington as judge, Nicholas Easton, John Coggeshall, and William Brenton as the three assistant elders, and William Dyer as secretary.[2] The place they had landed needed definition for possession. Free to design, they chose water as the most natural boundaries to the east, south and west, with a line five miles north across the land reaching from Narragansett Bay to the Atlantic Ocean. Searching for a name for the land thus defined, they thought of an English island, and called their landing "Newport", after the town of Newport on the Isle of Wight. Everywhere, Indian names were being changed for names of English heritage.

Again, William Dyer was assigned the job of surveying the territory, along with John Clarke and Nicholas Easton.[3] After each family was given ten acres of land, William Dyer carefully filed the Newport deeds along with the Pocasset deeds secretly in his possession. John Coggeshall, William Brenton, William Coddington and Nicholas Easton were assigned the larger points of land which still bear the names of their original owners. Mary and William Dyer took the land just south of Coddington Point and opposite Coasters Island for their farm.

Alongside the many exquisite arms of land reaching out onto Narragansett Bay, was a marsh which covered about two hundred acres on the western coast. The swamp, thickly interwoven with brambles and thickets, was a perfect hatching ground for mosquitoes.

Mary Dyer kept slapping herself all day and most of the night, but the persistent buzzing and bites continued. Never before had she been so bedeviled with such insects. A long skirt, shawl and cap were insufficient protection, for her entire body was covered with small red welts. William tried to smoke out their shelter at night, but there was little relief. Everyone suffered. It seemed as if the whole group would be devoured by the insidious sting of the mosquitoes. Once more the settlers had to resort to Indian wisdom.

One day while Nicholas Easton, Thomas Hazard and William Brenton were standing by Brenton's Cove discussing mosquitoes, some Indians from Conanicutt (Jamestown) came paddling around the bend. William Brenton signaled to them and they beached the canoes along the nearby shore.[4] With a contortion of language signs, combined with imitations of mosquitoes, the three Englishmen were able to communicate the problems of the marsh to the Indians, who nodded with understanding. Brenton felt the gaze of the Indians on him and soon realized they were admiring his magnificent navy blue overcoat, resplendent with large brass buttons, which he had brought

with him from England. One of the Indians gestured, "If you will
give me your coat, the pale face shall have the land made clear."
Brenton removed his coat and tried it on one of the startled Indians.
In response to grins and grunts, Brenton offered to give them the coat
in exchange for their clearing up the swamp. The Indians agreed to
the plan and returned to their canoe, swinging the coat. As they
paddled away to a remote cove, it occurred to Brenton that he might
never see the Indians or the coat again. He lingered around the point
for a while with Hazard and Easton, and just as they were about to
leave, the canoe reappeared with three grinning Indians wearing
necklaces made from the brass buttons they had removed from
Brenton's coat.

Now the Indians were ready to go to work on the swamp. First
they had to burn and clear out the underbrush. Then they dug furrows
for draining, and finally filled the former swamp with sand and
gravel until it was sufficiently firm for building lots, eventually
enough to accommodate fifty families, all for a dozen brass buttons.

The colonists also learned how the Indians used the land. It
became a challenge to combine these observations with their
knowledge of traditional English farming. It was the Indian women
who did their farming while the Indian men went hunting and
fishing.[5] Mary Dyer was fascinated to observe the proud English
farmers noting how the humble Indian women plowed their fields
using clam shells attached to sticks to dig furrows in the ground. As
the ground was fertile, they did not find it necessary to plow the
whole field. Instead, they plowed parallel furrows six feet apart,
crossplowing at the same interval. Interspersed with corn seeds, the
Indian women placed peas, beans and pumpkin seeds. From them the
English learned about multi-seed planting.[6]

The English farmers also learned how to be selective in the use of
grains. Instead of mixing them all together, as had been their former
custom, they planted barley, malt, and rye separately for the winter
feeding of sheep, sowed oats for their horses and wheat for domestic
use, always fertilizing their fields Indian fashion, with moose
manure, red seaweed, and fish scales.

Corn was the most important staple of all. The Indians described how a crow had flown to them with the first kernel of corn in its ear, which they planted and marveled as it grew and multiplied into "ears of corn." When the crow returned to menace the crops, they could not set bow and arrow on their sacred benefactor. Instead the Indians sent their children out in the fields at dawn to frighten the big black birds. As the children grew weary of this watch, they devised a substitute which they called a "scare crow."

Mary Dyer was glad the Indians had not been made to leave the southern tip of Aquidneck, as they had Pocasset, and she welcomed the opportunity to turn to these native Americans to learn about the truth of the land. God had sent these people ahead of the English. Mary loved any opportunity to relate to them. Every month of the year she could find them digging for shellfish on the shores adjacent to the Dyer farm. They showed her where to dig for oysters the size of a man's foot. Mary learned how to gather seaweed for a clambake. The Indians had a way of drawing enchantment out of the land. Mary observed them with gratitude.

Mary must have wondered how the English could have survived without the Indians to guide them in the wilderness. Could they have ever found their way through the dense forests without the well-trodden Indian paths to follow? Three times, Mary and William had turned to Indian skills for building temporary shelters. Would the Dyers have starved without learning from the Indians how to plant, hunt and fish? Mary was particularly interested in the Indian religion. They lived so close to the earth that they worshipped their surroundings, confusing the creations with the Creator. Mary understood this reverence for nature for she also felt the presence of God when she saw the white flashing of a deer's tail leaping into the deep dark woods.

Mary was distressed at leader Coddington's offensive attitude toward the Indians. An experienced administrator, and ambitious for Newport, Coddington differed greatly from Roger Williams, whose greatest desire was to be a friend and apostle to the Indians. Coddington was more concerned that the Indians should not interfere with the life of the white settlers, and he felt that it was necessary to make more stringent rules than Roger Williams.

On July 7, 1640, Coddington and his assistants called a meeting with Miantonomo and his sachems to discuss some of the rules.[7] It was agreed that Indians should not idle about the English settlement "except for trade, and messages, and in journey." Any Indian who did not depart from their houses when bidden should be punished. Mary Dyer could not abide this stark unfriendliness to those who had been so hospitable to the English. She had heard that Roger Williams, to the contrary, was putting up sixty Indians at a time in his house in Providence, and lending his canoe readily to them. Coddington, wanting to prevent any such borrowing of canoes, passed a law: "No Indian shall take any cannew from the English, neither from the boatside or shoreside, and the like not be done to them." Another of Coddington's concerns was the protection of livestock. Consequently, Indians were forbidden to hunt for deer or kill any cattle on their old hunting ground, Aquidneck.

It took a while for the Dyers to integrate their possessions. After a year of careful planning with the other first families of Newport, their sheep were all fenced in on the upper meadows, the cows around the farms, the oxen in a community enclosure, while the horses were left to forage in the woods. William Dyer was fortunate in having an island on which to park his hogs, while Brenton left his on Hog Island, just north of Dyer Island. Both Dyer and Brenton saw the possibilities of breeding hogs for commercial enterprises. There were good markets for bacon in Boston, Manhattan and Barbados, in exchange for rum, sugar, molasses and spices.

While William tended to the affairs of the world, Mary spent her time on the activities of the home.

Besides the preparation of food, a calendar full of chores awaited Mary's daily attention. The clothes they had brought from England sufficed for the first couple of years. By 1643, the Dyers had a pasture full of fluffy sheep. Many tedious steps lay between the shearing and final weaving of the yards and yards of cloth necessary for all the britches, vests, capes, shawls and skirts of different sizes and shapes required by her household.

The possession of so much more land for each family served to separate the women more than when they lived so closely together in

Boston. Mary had several friends who had also experienced living in the same three colonies. Dorothy Brenton, Marie Coggeshall and Mary Coddington were all tried and true friends. But Mary missed the vital, inspiring and spiritual friendship of Anne Hutchinson. The separation with Pocasset was so awkward to their relationship. The attitude of the men made it virtually impossible for her to dream of crossing the boundary line between the two separated communities. Mary looked askance at the important papers William held carefully in his safekeeping, cleverly arranging the records so that from them the Newport government should appear the only legitimate successor of the original compact. On the other side of the dividing line, Anne Hutchinson must have also shared some of the same sentiments of being torn away from her friend.

After a year of living apart, the inhabitants of Pocasset became quite aware that Newport was taking the lead. Anne Hutchinson was the first to suggest to her husband that the time was ripe to make some advances towards Newport. They should try and get together again. William Hutchinson was finally persuaded.

On arrival in Newport, William Hutchinson presented himself to William Coddington.[8] Coddington hurried to call together his General Court of Election. The Portsmouth contingent were very relieved to be "readily embraced" by the Newport inhabitants. They wasted no time in deciding that the two communities should be reunited. William Baulston was glad that he had thought to bring some of his best wine.

The assembled group discussed the Portsmouth Compact and their various falling outs. It was decided that the Indian name of Pocasset should be changed to honor the compact and that town should be renamed "Portsmouth." A seal was chosen to unite the two communities. A sheath of arrows bound up in leaves intertwined the engraved motto, "Amor vincait omnia."

In the process of reuniting Portsmouth and Newport, they decided to change some other names. The chief magistrate would no longer be "judge" but "governor." Instead of "magistrate," there would be "assistants." The governor would abide in Newport with two assistants and the deputy governor, with two more assistants, would represent Portsmouth. William Coddington was elected governor, with Nicholas Easton and John Coggeshall as his assistants. William Brenton, who had a residence in Portsmouth as well as Newport, was elected deputy governor, with William Hutchinson and John Porter as his assistants. The governors and assistants were invested with the office of justice of the peace.

It was decided that one court should meet in Newport on Tuesdays and another court would meet in Portsmouth on Thursdays. A joint treasury was voted, with equal amounts for each town. Robert Jeoffries was elected treasurer for Newport and William Baulston for Portsmouth. To ensure safety, an alarm system was devised by which drums would beat incessantly from plantation to plantation right up the coast in case of danger. Two barrels of gunpowder and thirty-two pikes were ready in the treasury at all times and soldiers met to train in the fields eight times a year. It took another meeting in Newport in May and one in Portsmouth in August to agree on everything they had to decide together. Everyone had to give a little, even Coddington, for Portsmouth insisted that no one should hold office for more than one year unless re-elected. Mary was ecstatic when she learned that all freemen were to be allowed free passage between the two settlements. At long last she would be able to reunite with her old friend.

As William Dyer collected all the records of their joint meetings and went about copying a Book of Law and Acts for Portsmouth, Mary looked over the contents of the papers with interest. She puzzled over one particular document. It was the deed signed on March 12, 1640, to reunite Newport and the newly-named Portsmouth. What drew Mary's attention was William's signature. Why had he signed his name Guliel Dyre on this particular document while he signed his name William Dyre on all the other documents. Mary recalled how they had signed the registry at St. Martins-in-the-Field after their marriage in 1633, "Marie Barrett and Guillaume Dyre." Was it his custom "to say it in French" for special occasions?

{ 12 }
News of Anne Hutchinson

Mary Dyer took the opportunity to have several visits with Anne Hutchinson during the two years following the reunion of Portsmouth and Newport. Anne appeared very disturbed by the persistent visits of the Boston authorities begging William Hutchinson to renounce the doctrine of his willful wife. William's repeated reply was, "That I shall not do; I am more nearly tied to my wife than the church, and I look upon her as a dear saint and a servant of God." William Hutchinson died in Portsmouth in 1642. After his death, Anne lost interest in Portsmouth. William had been her best friend, constant companion and devoted supporter. The Boston ministers continued to visit her and pursue her with religious questions. She needed a change of environment. Long Island looked like a good possibility.

Later in the year of 1642, Anne gathered together eight of her children and seven neighbors and moved to Long Island but this move did not prosper. With indefatigable energy, Anne again picked up her household of fifteen and moved to Dutch territory in Pelham Bay. There, she built a house near some other English settlers between a river and an Indian trail. At that time, the Hudson River Indians were in great conflict with the Dutch. It was their intention to kill all white settlers occupying their ancient land. Although Anne Hutchinson was very friendly with the Indians, this new house built so close to their trail looked like more Dutch trouble.

One August morning in the summer of 1643, Anne was planning to bake some blueberry pies. She asked her eight-year-old daughter, Susannah, to go out and pick some of the blueberries which were growing so plentifully in the neighboring woods. Susannah trotted off carrying her little Indian basket. Fifteen minutes later some Indians appeared at Anne's door and asked her to tie up her dogs. It seemed like a peculiar request for the dogs were lying around her yard, not bothering anyone. Anne's sons came to warn her that they had seen some Indians prowling about the woods. Anne started to call Susannah back. In a flash, Indians started to emerge by the dozens from the woods, surrounding her house. Anne's family and servants were boldly driven back into the house. As they struggled for freedom, each person was tied up. Anne watched the Indians bring forth their hatchets towards her dear ones. One by one they were butchered. Fourteen bodies were left wallowing in blood, some still groaning in pain. This was not enough for the Indians who proceeded to set the house on fire.

The neighbors heard the barking of the dogs, the screaming of the English, and the war cries of the excited Indians. Then they saw the leaping flames swallow up the wooden house. They hastily embarked in small boats to escape. Later they returned to investigate. They found the charred bodies of Anne (who was 52 years old), Francis, Anne II, Mary, Katherine, William, Zuryell and son-in-law, William Collins and their servants. The neighbors could not recognize the remains of any one person, so complete was the destruction.

Everyone assumed that her eight-year-old daughter, Susannah, had been among the charred bodies in the house. But Susannah, who had been out picking berries in the woods, was kidnapped by the Indians as they retreated, and she lived with them for two years. When she was returned to her remaining family in Boston, she spoke only the Indian tongue.

The Boston magistrates and preacher John Wilson did not grieve to hear that Anne Hutchinson had been butchered and burned to death. Instead, they rejoiced that God had seen fit to smite the woman they had banished.

It was ironic that the Indians chose to slaughter Anne Hutchinson. Six years earlier when John Wilson was chosen to lead a battalion and join the Narragansetts to fight the Pequots, Anne Hutchinson had used all of her ingenuity to persuade her Antinomian followers against going to war.

This event gave a turnabout twist to the prevailing opinion that the English invaders were generally the guilty ones in taking cruel advantage of the Native Americans. For Mary Dyer, who had confidence in the Indians, it must have been a disillusioning disaster.

Mary Dyer never quite got over Anne's death. Mary had missed Anne her first three years in Newport. Anne's spiritual intensity, her adventurous ideas, her confident, stubborn statements, and her expressed joy in life had brought inspiration and hope to Mary's first years in the colonies. After the shared disasters of the "monster births," Mary longed for the companionship of Anne when her healthy baby daughter was born the first year in Newport. The other Newport wives were nice women and pleasant people for sharing daily chores — Elizabeth Clarke, Dorothy Brenton, Mary Cogge-shall and Mary Coddington were good neighbors — but the lightning was missing.

Mary conducted a service for Anne in Providence at the home of Anne's sister, Catherine Scott. There were five remaining Hutchinson children: Faith, who married Thomas Savage and lived in Boston; Bridget, who married John Sanford and lived in Rhode Island; Edward, whose daughter Anne later married Samuel Dyer, and Richard, living in Boston. Susannah was still living with the Pequot Indians at the time of Mary's service for Anne.

More than any of the surviving members of the Hutchinson family, Mary Dyer inherited Anne Hutchinson's message to the world. She was determined that it should not be snuffed out in the dust of Pelham.

13. Statue of Anne Hutchinson with her daughter Susannah by
Cyrus Dallin, with the inscription commemorating Anne's utterance
as she left the Boston Church:
The Lord judgeth not as man judgeth.
Better to be cast out of the church
Than to deny Christ.
(courtesy of Massachusetts State House Library):

{ 13 }
First Charter for Rhode Island

During the 1640s, there was a great deal of travelling between London, Boston, and Newport. Men kept moving between these three pivotal points by brig, shallop, horse, or foot to argue their religious differences, battle their territorial rights and trade their respective wares. It was a triangle of tension.

One of the great concerns was over the possession of land. The Royal Charter for Massachusetts had set quite clear boundaries. However, Aquidneck and Providence Plantations had no sanction from England for the land they occupied by purchase from the Narragansett Indians, and their only constitution was the one they had written for themselves. The other colonies were continually tempted to challenge their right to such a desirable location. Although they accepted religious dissidents readily, the very essence of their freedom suddenly appeared shaky without the blessing of a royal charter. Roger Williams elected to go to England to procure the necessary document in 1642.

As Roger was refused entrance to the port of Boston, as a departure point, he appealed to the Dutch and obtained passage on a ship sailing from New Amsterdam. During his rough sea voyage, he managed to write Key Into the Language of America. Roger reported that it was composed as "a lump at sea" to aid his memory as well as introduce the language and customs of the Native Americans to the English. Once in London, it was published by Gregory Dexter in 1643, attracting so much favorable attention in Parliament that it served to hasten the granting of a charter for Rhode Island.

More controversial was the next document he wrote while in London addressed to John Cotton in protest for his exile from

Boston, The Bloody Tenet of Persecution (a conference between Truth and Peace). In it he wrote: "Every man has a right, as a citizen, to hold any opinions and to practice any ceremonies, which he please, unless he disturbs the civil power." Roger was successful in receiving a civic patent for "The Providence Plantation and Rhode Island." He stayed in London until the Bloody Tenet was published and returned to Providence in 1644, complete with the Charter, his publisher, Gregory Dexter, and a letter from Parliament to the Boston authorities requesting a welcome landing for Roger at the port of Boston.

When Roger Williams approached his home he was met by a dozen Indian canoes paddling down the Seekonk River to welcome him. The people of Providence Plantation and Aquidneck were also rejoicing at the return of Roger Williams. But there was one very reluctant citizen.

In the joint colony of Newport and Portsmouth on the island of Aquidneck, William Coddington had been re-elected as Governor each year from 1639 to 1647. He was the wealthiest man in Newport and a leader in commerce as well as Government. From his earlier experiences in Lincolnshire, he had brought knowledge of farming and raising cattle. He owned the most land and had the necessary assets to develop surplus in timber, livestock, and corn. With Portsmouth and Newport flourishing under his guidance, Coddington had every intention of drawing a ring around Aquidneck and the adjoining islands and calling them his own forevermore.

Coddington's plan for an exclusive island colony was first tested in 1644, when Roger Williams returned from his expedition to England with the civic patent for "Providence Plantation and Rhode Island."[1] At the same time, the raucous Samuel Gorton, who had been made to feel unwelcome in Boston, Plymouth, and Aquidneck, had purchased from Miantonomo the point of land between Providence and Aquidneck, called Shawowmet. And while Roger Williams was receiving his Royal Charter, Samuel Gorton was also in London persuading the Earl of Warwick to secure him a Royal Charter. On his return he changed the Indian name of Shawowmet to Warwick and persuaded Roger Williams to attach Warwick to

Providence Plantations. For three years Coddington tried to oppose this union of Providence Plantations and Warwick with his treasured island.

In 1647, the union of the four colonies under the Roger Williams charter was finally accomplished. After seven years as Governor, William Coddington had to step down while John Coggeshall took over the office.

The first meeting of the united colonies took place May 19-21, 1647 in Portsmouth. Delegates from Providence Plantations and Warwick paddled their canoes across Narragansett Bay, hugging the shores of Prudence Island as a shelter from the sharp spring winds, while the delegates from Newport arrived on horseback.

John Coggeshall's first act as Governor was to choose an anchor as an insignia for Providence Plantations and Rhode Island, and "Hope" as the motto for the newly united colony of Providence, Warwick, Portsmouth, and Newport. His next act was to try and legalize all they were hoping for. He assigned John Clarke to write a Code of Laws in 1647 declaring the inviolability of freedom of conscience.[2] John Clarke called on William Dyer to assist him in writing the document.

William Coddington did not share the satisfaction of others in all that had been accomplished in the Portsmouth meeting of 1647. He simply could not accept his loss of leadership. In the midst of his political difficulties, he lost his wife, Mary. She was his second wife to die of illness in America. Once again he would have to return to England for a suitable replacement. The people of Newport were so relieved to be rid of Coddington for a while that they did not question his reason for going.

14. Going to Church (courtesy of Bettmann Archives).

{ 14 }
Quelling The Quest

It was William Dyer's privilege to work side by side with John Clarke as surveyor of land and inventor of words to establish the foundation for a new community. The designs of their lives were sketched in the laws they wrote together. Creating laws in Newport was far more challenging and satisfying than selling capes and daggers in London.

Mary had never seen William so ebullient as that night in 1647 when he came home carrying the first Body of Laws, written in assistance to John Clarke. Mary read and reread the precious words.

"All MEN may walk as their conscience persuade them, every one in the name of God." Where was the cool draft coming from, the mysterious funnel of discontent which prevented Mary from identifying with the total joy of her husband" Unlike William, Mary was not convinced by the written word as the final expression of the truth. She sought a closer look at human experience. And that closer look alerted her to the reality that all women were not afforded the same privilege "to walk as their conscience persuade them, every one in the name of God."

Everywhere the privileges were spelled out for men, while women's rights remained indistinct. In the exuberance of fulfilling their own ambitions, it never occurred to the men that the special needs of women were being ignored. Accustomed to the pattern, the ladies remained complacent, conforming to the masculine interpretation of freedom of religion. There was no law to legitimize the expression by women and no incentive for asking questions. Except for an unusually bright, perceptive woman like Mary Dyer.

Mary had some reservations about the leaders of Rhode Island, so whole-heartedly respected by her husband William, who thought John Clarke was the most inspired person he had ever met. Mary wanted to share William's admiration, but she could not forget how Clarke had exposed Anne Hutchinson to calamity when he wrote to Governor Winthrop describing the distorted delivery that would have been Anne's fourteenth child.[1] Moreover, John Cotton had chosen to use John Clarke's gynecological description of the mishap as a subject for one of his lectures to his Boston congregation.

Mary would have felt easier about John Clarke if he had limited his services to minister and statesman, but he was also her physician. When she arrived in Newport, already "expecting," there were no other experienced mid-wives nearby. Frightened that she might repeat her Boston experience of delivering a deformed daughter, Mary could not help worrying that in the event, Clarke would betray her as he had Anne. Somehow, she could not vent this private fear to William, who sincerely believed that John Clarke could do no wrong.

As the religious leader of the group that first landed in Pocasset and later founded Newport, John Clarke introduced an entirely different concept of baptism to the group, "I testifie that Baptism, or dipping is one of the Commandments of the Lord Jesus —Dipping is not sprinkling. To dip is to plunge under water, as it were to drown but yet as with safety, so the party may be drowned again and again."[2] While attending the University of Leyden in Holland he became interested in the Anabaptist movement, which had sprung up as an offshoot of the Baptist Church in Zurich in 1523. Although their religion was based on the five Calvinistic clauses similar to those of the Congregational Church, the Anabaptists added a sixth clause which changed the whole concept of baptism. The Anabaptists believed that infant baptism was scripturally unwarranted and that baptism should be restricted to the total immersion of regenerate Christians. This interpretation was unacceptable to the Puritans and they passed a law in 1644 stating that anyone who opposed the baptism of infants would be sentenced to banishment (but not whipping).[3] Not everyone in Newport believed in John Clarke's Baptist principles but he was the only minister of the only church and submersion in water was not a prerequisite to join. Every Sunday the community gathered at the little wooden church overlooking Newport Harbor to hear John Clarke pronounce such congenial sentiments as, "Every believer should improve the talent the Lord has given him for the edification of the whole.... No one has the liberty to restrain or compel another to worship God.... When bodies are present through fear, hearts and minds are not changed."[4] John Clarke spoke like an apostle. He was the leader the people had been waiting for. Mary wished with all her heart that she could be as totally satisfied as the rest of the community.

William had another friend whose views concerned Mary much more than John Clarke's. Roger Williams was given credit for being the original liberator of religious freedom. Mary appreciated that he was responsible for the unheard of step of separating Church and State in Rhode Island. He had opened the doors of Providence and Newport to all dissident religions, and Mary would have liked to acclaim this hero, but again she found herself with reservations. It was Samuel Gorton who had told her that, in Salem, where Roger Williams had spent two years as preacher before fleeing to Providence, he had insisted that the women adopt the Muslim custom of wearing veils in church, preaching that "The Lord hath given a covering of longer hair to women as a sign or teacher of Covering, Modesty, and Bashfulness, Silence and Retardedness, and therefore women are not fitted for many actions and employments." Roger justified his attitude by saying that subjection of wives to their husbands was an ordinance of God.

Mary knew that she was unusually fortunate in not only being adored, but also respected by William. (Many other men were writing letters to England boasting about the law that forbid wives to be beaten or to be treated like servants.) Mary shuddered at the desired image of the silent, bashful woman, immobilized from responding to the challenging possibilities in the new world. She had special concern for Mary Williams, the woman who could not write her own name, married to the man who could speak seven languages. There were other punishments more subtle than whipping.

Roger Williams broke with the Salem Church the winter of his banishment. He pronounced all members of the Church "unregenerate,"[5] because they had not made a complete severing of their ties with the Church of England. Mary Williams and her daughters continued to attend the bi-weekly meetings to which they were accustomed. Roger declared that they were therefore unregenerate and unfit to communicate with God. As a result, Mary Williams and the children were not allowed to be present while Roger gave his blessing before every meal, thanking God for the food Mary had so lovingly prepared.

Mary Dyer was not the only person stunned by the ridiculous behavior of such an esteemed man. Thomas Hooker, who had engaged in debates with Roger Williams on other occasions, took the opportunity to give Roger a well-deserved joshing, saying, "If it be unlawful to call an unregenerate person to pray, since it is an action of God's worship, then it is unlawful for your unregenerate child to pray for a blessing upon his own meat. If it be unlawful for him to pray for a blessing upon his meat, it is unlawful for him to eat it, it is sanctified by prayer and without prayer unsanctified. If it be unlawful for him to eat it, it is unlawful for you to call upon him to eat it, for it is unlawful for you to call upon him to sin."[6]

Roger Williams considered that women were predestined to be the weaker vessel. God had designed the world like a watch with the large hour hand controlled by men and the tiny minute hand by women, who were only equipped to care for their homes and children, but not to participate as apostles, teachers or preachers. Roger Williams entertained an exception to his theory, saying that there were some women that God preferred before thousands of men, especially those born of special favor like Queen Elizabeth. "Yet," he maintained, "such a law does not destroy the order, which God hath set in bounds and distinctions between male and female."[7] Mary found it hard to believe what Roger said " that only such women as Queens should be given the liberty to express themselves. How could he receive the multitude of assorted religions with such favor and still disregard the qualifications of the opposite sex"

In an age when, for some, the beginnings of scientific thought were loosening religious superstitions, Mary was forever asking questions and looking for the truth. She was perhaps the only person of her time to experience the beginnings of so many different religious sects, and yet she had no opportunity to express her convictions. She had moved from the Anglican Church in England, sampled the Puritan Church in Boston, and chosen to go with the Antinomians to Rhode Island where the Anabaptist Church was just taking root. Still unsatisfied, Mary continued to explore.

During the 1640s, Mary spent most of her time bearing and rearing a family. By 1650, Samuel was 15, and little Mary 10 years old; Will, named after his father (as had their first-born buried in England) was nine; next came Maher, a nickname for his real biblical name, Mahershallaber; then two-year-old Henry (possibly named after Sir Harry Vane) while the youngest was Charles, born in 1650, just after the execution of Charles I and ten years before Charles II came to the throne. During this time of childrearing and homemaking, Mary had been treading water in her ideological space, diving from time to time into the depths of religious inquiry, but returning without satisfaction to a life which sapped her vitality and distracted her quest for spiritual composure. She could not forget the highs and lows of her days in Boston. The Antinomians had experienced such exuberance when women and men were sharing together new meanings of God's message to the world. The political cut-off had served to interfere. But worst of all was Mary's personal experience of being censored and damned by the whole world because of the unfortunate birth over which she had no control. Her experience during those three years had sharpened her sensitivities to all mankind. Mary was listening for a message too universal to be stored away.

After the birth of her sixth child in 1650, Mary's quest for a more encompassing religion was beginning to overshadow her family responsibilities. Her role of total dedication to her own family was not enough for this woman who was called to nurture the greater family of mankind. Confused by the conflict, her prayers reassured her that her immediate family would be well cared for if she ventured forth beyond Dyer Farm.

The people of Newport were always on the lookout for news from England, which took a tantalizing amount of time to be delivered.

When Captain Trevice docked in the Newport Harbor in the early 1650s, everyone was in for a shock. Civil War had broken out in England upon the execution of King Charles I in 1649. The House of Commons had abolished the monarchy and established a "Commonwealth of Free State," and a Council of State had been created by the purged Parliament. Sir Oliver Cromwell had been elected "Protector." It seemed hard to imagine England, without a King or Queen, three thousand miles away. Despite the many reservations over the rule of King Charles I, everyone was startled and concerned for the mother country.

Captain Trevice stayed for a few months in Newport refurbishing his ship. It was the custom for the people of Newport to line up on the shore and wave farewells to any parting ship on its way to England. As Captain Trevice set sail someone noticed the jaunty figure of Mary Dyer standing on the deck. She was obviously alone. The unanswerable question was how could she be undertaking this perilous trip across the ocean leaving William and their six children behind? The question has not been satisfactorily answered during three centuries of inquiry. Whether or not the immediate news of the King's assassination could have in some way affected her personal life in London — we do not know. We can think of a few possible reasons for this most unexpected departure, but they remain only speculations.

{ 15 }
Coddington's Disaster

W hen William Coddington arrived in London just after the execution of Charles I, England was in a state of confusion, with Oliver Cromwell trying to establish himself as the Great Protector. Coddington looked up his old friend from Boston days, Sir Harry Vane, who, as a member of Parliament, was able to introduce him to Cromwell. It took time for him to interest the frenzied Council of State in events taking place overseas.

Oliver Cromwell, Sir Harry Vane, and John Milton, as Secretary of Foreign Affairs, were united in their support of an independent Rhode Island. Although they were aware of friction, they had no way of knowing that Coddington was not backed by the rest of Rhode Island in his special request. As a result, they annulled the charter granted Roger Williams in 1643 and gave Coddington his own private charter. The preamble stated that William Coddington was to be Governor of Aquidneck and Conanicutt for life, with full powers to, "Exercise the government of the said islands and cause the equal and indifferent justice to be duly administered." Aquidneck (Newport and Portsmouth) was to be separated from Providence Plantations and Warwick.

By 1651, Coddington had not only secured a new charter, but also a new wife, and by then a new son. His third wife was Anne Brinley. At the same time Coddington was courting Anne, Nathaniel Sylvester, who had just returned from purchasing Shelter Island in Long Island Sound, was wooing her younger sister, Gissell.

Early in 1651, Nathaniel Sylvester and William Coddington secured a barque, the Swallow, to transport their brides to their American islands, stopping on their way in Barbados to admire

Coddington's well-bred stallions turning wheels of the sugar mills. It was a rough voyage and as they neared the coast of Aquidneck, the sea was high with rollers, and stormy winds were increasing. Entering Newport Harbor, the barque was driven by unexpected fresh gusts of wind onto the rocks of the island of Conanicutt. The Swallow pounded on the relentless granite and started to split apart. William Coddington and Nathaniel Sylvester made a gallant rescue of their wives before the ship splintered. Once their lives had been saved, the Brinley sisters watched with horror while their precious English household possessions were dashed to pieces by the breakers.

A shallop rescued the shipwrecked party and sailed them across to Newport. Shivering, frightened, and disheartened, the Brinley sisters landed in America, Anne to lead one life on Aquidneck and Gissell to pursue another on Shelter Island. Both Brinley sisters were to become important in the life of Mary Dyer.

When Coddington arrived in Newport, waving his patent which established him as their ruler for life, the people of Rhode Island could hardly believe it. It seemed as if Coddington had opened the door to a hurricane which was about to destroy what he had originally designed. Did he intend to have the Portsmouth Patent ripped to pieces? Had he forgotten how they had all worked together to establish a democratic government? Coddington had betrayed them in misrepresenting their interests to Sir Harry Vane and the Council of State. To hold the office of Governor for life would be absolutely unacceptable.

Roger Williams, John Clarke, William Dyer, Henry Bull, Nicholas Easton, John Coggeshall, and William Brenton all met to consider what they could do. They tried to get Coddington to give up his claim as permanent Governor, but he would only shake the parliamentary patent in their faces. For a while there were two separate governments, one on the Providence mainland and one on the island of Aquidneck. Protests escalated from the throwing of rocks to the showing of guns in Newport. Life became so unbearable for William Coddington and his new wife, Anne Brinley, that they were forced to flee to Boston for the winter.

The concerned citizens of Rhode Island decided that the only solution to their dilemma would be to send a commission to London to get the disastrous patent nullified. Roger Williams and John Clarke were chosen to go. When William Dyer was asked to accompany John Clarke as secretary, he was more than willing to join them. Not only did he want to bring back a new charter, but hoped in his heart to return with his wife. The three men set sail from Boston in 1651.[1]

15. Coaster Island and the Dyer farm 350 years later
(photo by John Hopf).

{16}
With William Dyer, 1651-1657

When Roger Williams, John Clarke, and William Dyer arrived in London, they, like Coddington before them, wasted no time in contacting their good friend, Sir Harry Vane. Although Sir Harry's mistaken support of the Coddington Charter had made their trip necessary, their respect for him remained unchanged. Roger Williams relied on Sir Harry unswervingly and always referred to him as, "the sheet anchor of our ship." As a member of Parliament, Sir Harry was working closely with the Lord Protector, Oliver Cromwell, and John Milton as the Secretary of Foreign Affairs. All three supported a democratic charter for Rhode Island.

Parliament had other priorities. The Netherlands might represent the model of ideological freedom which England was trying to attain, but economically, England was being undercut by Holland on the high seas. The Dutch had a corner on transportation at a time when England was suffering from the results of Civil War. The Dutch bottoms had monopolized the "carrying trade" with the colonies, and in order to counteract this commercial handicap, England passed the First Navigation Act of 1651. This provided that only British ships could transport British goods; other countries would have to supply their own ships for transportation of their own goods. Ships were boarded and searched to make sure they were complying with the Navigation Act. The Dutch resisted this Act and war broke out between England and Holland in 1652. When Admiral Blake was defeated by Admiral Van Trip in the English Channel, the priorities of Rhode Island's charter dropped even lower on the list of issues concerning Parliament.

This gave William Dyer some time to spend with Mary. They had many friends and relatives that they had not seen for sixteen years, but Mary was most interested in a new religious sect which had become very popular in England. The Seekers were made up of people who had broken away from the Anglican Church and had become dissatisfied with the Puritan response. They were looking for a different method of worship better adapted to their spiritual wants and they served as recipients for the religiously restless and unsatisfied, leaving new possibilities open to a variety of believers. Their motto must have had great appeal to such an adventurer as Mary Dyer: "Better not to stand still, but keep searching with an open mind!"

Mary was eager to have William join her as a participant of the Seeker meetings in the fields on the outskirts of London. He attended several, but he did not share Mary's conviction, his own interests being diverted by the activities of Parliament and his mission to rescind Coddington's Charter. William had been such an ardent Antinomian in Boston that it must have been very disappointing to Mary to have him only lukewarm over the Seekers.

After a year of distraction with his naval duties on the English Channel, Sir Harry Vane persevered and was successful in getting Parliament to annul the very charter he had naively gotten passed two years previously.

It was important to dispatch the good news back to Newport as quickly as possible. Roger Williams and John Clarke had further business to attend to in London, and William Dyer became the logical messenger. He hurried to Bristol to inquire about the first possible passage to America. He found Captain Christen on the docks getting his ship ready to set sail for Newport. The boat was well-loaded, but Captain Christen made room for another passenger. William had hoped that Mary would be returning from London with him but she was not ready to leave England so soon. She wanted to meet the man, referred to as the King of Seekers, George Fox, who was reported to have created a religion of his own, called Quakers. Reluctantly, William left Mary in London, and sailed off with Captain Christen, hoping that his wife would soon return home to her family.

Ten weeks later, there were shouts of excitement in the streets of Newport when an approaching ship was spotted late the afternoon of February 18, 1653. The Coggeshalls, Brentons, Bulls, and anyone around, hastened to the icy shores of the harbor in anticipation. Nothing caused more excitement than news from England. The barque was blurred by snow flurries, but one could see the rigging was swollen with cold and the bowsprit burdened with icicles. Drifts of snow kept spilling from the spritsails as the ice-clad ship pushed her way into the harbor. Captain Christen was the first to shiver ashore, his boots crunching on the frozen mixture of snow, salt, and sand. William Dyer came bounding behind him, eager with news. He was received with jubilation as he read the message from the Council of State rescinding the Coddington Commission and reaffirming the former charter. William Dyer also had a letter to read from Roger Williams.[1] Bonfires were lit in the main square of Newport as more and more people gathered to hear the warming news.

The day after his illustrious landing in Newport, William Dyer was busy communicating the news to the inhabitants of Portsmouth, Providence, and Warwick. William Dyer wrote an accompanying letter, February 19, 1653:

Loving Friends and Neighbours,

These are to signify unto you that it hath pleased the Right Honorable Council of State, authorised by the Supreme Authority of the Committee of England, to betrust myself with letters and orders concerning the Colony, and the Welfare thereof.

Be pleased to understand that upon Tuesday come seven nights at Portsmouth in Rhode Island att Mr. Baulston's House, I shall be there (God willing) ready to attend the communication of the trust committed to my charge, unto all such Free inhabitants as shall there make therein personal appearances.

On March 1, freemen from the four towns met in Portsmouth and reinstated the officers who had been displaced by the Coddington Commission, to serve until the next election. William Coddington was forced to make a public repentance. He then retired from public life to his farming enterprises.

Except for the Coddingtons and a few of their loyal supporters, the relief was universal over the rescission of the Coddington Charter. For two years, the threat of oligarchy had weakened the health of the Rhode Island democracy. There was much rejoicing that the alarm was over. William Dyer was triumphant.

But after the initial exhilaration of his political success, he had some sobering realities to face in reestablishing life on his farm, which had been cared for by a tenant farmer in his absence. He needed more help. He also needed to change the way he recruited workers. In 1649, William Wittingham had introduced slave labor from Barbados, and the community also drew from the supply of indentured Pequot Indians. Although William Dyer and his compatriots desperately needed labor on the Rhode Island farms, they early recognized that slavery could not co-exist with democracy. Their households should not contradict their ideals. In 1652, the first gesture towards the abolition of slavery was made in Newport when a law was passed limiting to ten years the service of any indentured servants who had helped to start the first farms in Newport in the early 1640s.[2]

William must have missed Mary, but his son, Samuel, was a knowledgeable farmer and took over a lot of the responsibility on the Dyer farm. Samuel married Anne Hutchinson's granddaughter, Anne, and she was a great help in assisting little Mary with the care of the younger boys.

Of his 87 acres of land on Aquidneck, Dyer allotted 20 acres for grazing. One of the most effective improvements for better farming was the importation of English grass, which was far superior to Rhode Island grass. John Coggeshall went into the business of importing English grass seed, and sold it to the other farmers for five shillings a bushel. It took three bushels to plant an acre. The lush green superior grass, which had so recently replaced whole acres of brambles and swamps, was neatly enclosed by palisade fencing.

The greatest change in the working life of every single man in Newport took place in 1656, when Henry Leonard and Ralph Russell set up the Raynham Forge in Taunton. Iron hoes and shovels replaced crude Indian makeshifts; chains replaced rope pulleys for oxen hauling logs and for housewives pulling up buckets of water from the well; leather door hinges were replaced by iron; and barrels were forged for guns. Besides the advantages for farming, the Raynham Forge produced many aids for shipping, with fittings for the vessels, and, most important, anchors that would hold. Boats could sail from Newport right up the Taunton River to pick up iron and transport it back to Newport.

By 1653, the Rhode Islanders felt it necessary to take active measures against the Dutch who were sending exploring parties and making claims in Long Island Sound. The General Assembly of Providence Plantations granted privateer commissions to John Underhill, Edward Hall, and William Dyer, "to go against the Dutch."[3] Dyer was given charge of the expeditions by sea and Underhill by land. Dyer threw himself into the adventure of plundering Dutch bottoms. It was made even more congenial by the excitement of his twelve-year-old son, Will, who was an excellent swimmer. He had spent much of his boyhood diving for sea treasures in Narragansett Bay, and was as helpful a son by sea as Samuel was by land.

As the Colonies had no navy, Dutch boats were captured and refitted for the use of privateers. William Dyer acquired such a ship with its flat stern, so different from the rounded sterns of the English ships to which he was accustomed.

To capture a Dutch ship, father and son would wait off the Long Island shore until all on board were asleep. Then, they would slip a canoe over the side of their own boat, and, quietly, paddle close to the desired "bottom." With a length of rope tied around his waist, Will would dive off the canoe, swim beneath the Dutch boat and strangle the Dutch rudder with his rope. He then returned to his father's canoe which they would paddle back to their ship hidden in a nearby cove. As the sun rose the next morning, father and son would eagerly watch the Dutch attempting to set sail, completely baffled by what had happened to their ship. While the Dutch struggled in confusion the Dyers would sail over, board the ship, and demand that any other-than-Dutch goods be handed over. William had a badge to certify his authority as a privateer. Father and son returned loaded with British and French treasures. Everything they seized was reported to Robert Earle of Newport. The assortment of captured prizes became a subject of controversy among the other colonies. Providence and Warwick protested that these commissions were "illegal and like to set all New England on fire." Dyer and Underhill should have no such liberty of action. There were more complaints and court proceedings from Plymouth, Massachusetts, and Connecticut. The privateers were finally forced to give up their adventures against the Dutch, and not long afterwards the war with Holland came to a close in 1654.

During the first two years after his return to Newport, William Dyer missed the companionship and support of his good friends, John Clarke and Roger Williams. In 1654 when Roger Williams finally returned to Providence, William Dyer was relieved.

Roger Williams was distressed at the dissension he found when he returned. He turned to the sea for a metaphor to help him express how he felt when addressing his people:

Well-beloved friends and neighbors, I am like a man in a great fog. I know not well how to steer. I fear to run upon the rocks at home, having had trails abroad. I fear to run quite backward, as men in a mist do, and undo all that I have been time undoing myself to keep up the names of a people, a free people, not enslaved to [the] bondages and iron yokes [nor] to the divisions and disorders within ourselves.[4]

The quarreling in Rhode Island had also caused great dismay in England. Sir Harry Vane had given Roger Williams a letter to take back with him to the people of Rhode Island. England was ever ready to look over the shoulder of events in the colonies. Sir Harry Vane wrote:

How is it that there are such divisions among you? Headiness, tumults, disorders and injustice? The noise echoes in ears of all, as well friends as enemies, by every return of shipps from those parts. Is not the fear and awe of God amongst you to rest. Is not the love of Christ in you, to fill you with yearning bowels toward another, and constrain you not to yourselves, but He that died for you, yea and is risen again? Are there no wise men among you? No public self-denying spirits that at least ... can find out some way of reconciliation ... amongst yourselves. The Counsil of State gave you your fredom, ... supporting a better use would be made of it.... But I hope better things will come from you ... silence your enemies, encourage your friends and honor the name of God, which of love hath much blasphemy by reason of you.[5]

Despite all the difficulties in Providence Plantations, Newport was growing in every way. The spiritual outreach encouraged Jews from Manhattan, who had become discordant with the Dutch, and others from Curaçoa to find asylum in Newport where they founded the first Jewish Synagogue in America.[6] Agriculture, mercantile, and marine pursuits were coordinated to ship hogs, cattle, sheep and maize all over the world in exchange for other necessities. William Dyer as Attorney General for Rhode Island from 1650-1653 played an integral part in the multi-sided growth. He was a highly respected citizen throughout the Colonies and also very much loved, referred to so often in the literature as "dear Mr. Dyer." William was largely content; his children were gainfully occupied; the sheep were in the pasture; the horses were in the stable; the oxen were in the commons; the hogs were on Dyer Island; but there was still that empty space next to him in his bed. In his semi-sleep, he would reach for the beloved body, only to be awakened by emptiness. What was Mary doing lingering in England for so long?

{ 17 }
Swarthmore Hall, 1654-57

Mary's true purpose in leaving her family and going to England is not known, and there is no record of how she spent all seven years. We do know she became an ardent Quaker and that she attended meetings of the "Seekers" in the early 1650s. From this time on, her spiritual search dominated her life. We know that she met George Fox who founded a new religion, and because it caused its members to "quake and tremble before the Lord" this sect was called Quakers.[1] Swarthmore Hall was the main Quaker meeting place and Sir Harry Vane was the most likely person to introduce Mary to the Fells, who owned Swarthmore Hall. One can imagine what a thrilling adventure it must have been for Mary. Unfortunately, she kept no journal so we have to rely on the Swarthmore manuscripts and George Fox's Journal to relate her experiences.

Sir Harry Vane was one of Mary's oldest and best friends. After helping William Dyer, Roger Williams, and John Clarke annul the Coddington Charter, Sir Harry continued to fight for democratic values. But by 1654 he left Parliament because of his bitter disagreement with Sir Oliver Cromwell over Sir Harry's proposal to give people of all faiths the right to vote. Cromwell was in a rage when the bill was passed. Although he believed in freedom of religion, he could not tolerate the vote of the Roman Catholics or the free-wheeling "Ranters". It was a dramatic moment for Parliament when Cromwell stood up and screamed at the top of his lungs, "Lord, deliver me from Sir Harry Vane!"

After this confrontation with Cromwell, Sir Harry and Lady Vane, accompanied by their seven children, moved from London to

Belleau, their country home in Lincolnshire. This elegant manor served as open house for friends coming from America; Roger Williams spent several weeks at a time before his return to Providence in 1654. It is most likely that Mary Dyer also visited Belleau. We may guess she confided in Sir Harry her interest in meeting the famous George Fox and that he gave her an introduction to Judge Thomas Fell, a fellow member of the Long Parliament and the owner of a manor in Ulverston, called "Swarthmore Hall," which had recently become the Quaker meeting place for George Fox.

It took several days to ride to Cumbria on the northwestern coast of England. Mary would have had to wait for the tide to recede before crossing Morecomb Bay to Ulverston. It is easy to imagine what might happen on such a journey. She was not experienced in the art of riding through quicksand. When her horse stumbled and slid into the treacherous ground, she had to pull on the bridle reins with all her might until, finally, exhausted, horse and rider extracted themselves from the sucking sands to the more reliable land. Preferring to walk the last mile from the Ulverston Market to Swarthmore Hall, Mary dismounted.

Swarthmore Hall stood like a castle on a hill midway between the sea and the moors with a spectacular view of Morecomb Bay to the north and Osmothaly Moors to the east. Approaching the top of the hill, Mary could see the three-storied manor built of grey freestone and roofed with the local slate that complemented the greys and greens of the surrounding country. Barns and stables protected the windward side of the manor. On the leeward side she could see an elderly figure digging a hole in the ground. His formal attire and erect stance did not give him the appearance of a gardener. As Mary walked closer, she realized that this must be Judge Fell. She was timid in introducing herself as a stranger on his property, but when Mary mentioned Sir Harry Vane, the Judge was welcoming and reassured her that he was accustomed to Quaker visitors. As he shook the small yew tree he was planting, he explained that it was for Rachel, their newborn seventh daughter. He pointed with pride to six other yew trees of ascending heights all planted in a row by the side of the house to celebrate the birth of each successive daughter. The

Judge patted down his last shovelful of dirt and invited Mary into the house.

Mary entered the manor and was shown into a panelled living room with a large stone fireplace and magnificent bay window, three stories high, overlooking Morecomb Bay. Margaret Fell was there to greet her, and her exuberant warmth melted any feelings of strangeness. Gathering her red cape around her, she sat down next to Mary, in anticipation of conversation. As she started to talk about the Quaker movement, she was joined by one daughter after another, all echoing her enthusiasm. Each girl was aspiring to become a Quaker leader like their mother.

Margaret Fell confided in Mary Dyer that it was George Fox who was most responsible for her faith and activities. She confessed, "George Fox opened us a book we had never read in, nor indeed had never heard that it was our duty to read in, [to wit] the light of Christ in our conscience, our minds, never being turned towards it before."[2] He had encouraged Margaret Fell to be the woman she did not know existed, releasing her completely from a tradition of meekness, obedience, and silence by showing his appreciation of her qualities as a woman. Fox inspired her to speak up in meetings and exercise her spiritual gifts, and she, in turn, was trying to encourage younger women to realize themselves in the same way.

Mary Dyer wondered how Margaret Fell had ever met George Fox, living as she did in an elegant house on top of a remote hill on the wild northwestern coast of England. Margaret Fell told her that George Fox had arrived at Swarthmore Hall on an afternoon when Judge Fell was away on a Welsh circuit and Margaret was shopping in town. The servants had answered the knock at the door and George Fox had entered to find all the Fell daughters in conversation with William Lampitt, the visiting priest from the local Puritan Church. In an attempt to explain his presence, George Fox got into a heated discussion with Priest Lampitt. The children were shaken by the intensity of their arguments. When Margaret Fell returned, her elder daughter went hurrying to meet her at the front door, whispering that a man had arrived who disagreed bitterly with their good friend the priest. Margaret Fell walked apprehensively into the flagstone living room to confront the interloper. The moment she met George Fox, she was spellbound. The priest left and George Fox was invited to dinner. That evening Fox talked at length with Margaret Fell, her children and their servants.

Everyone at Swarthmore Hall was so inspired by his message that Margaret persuaded Fox to stay over and speak to the people of Ulverston in the local church the following Sunday. George Fox was as charismatic in the Ulverston Church as at Swarthmore Hall. Priest Lampitt was very upset by the presence of this magnetic man and the town soon became divided between those who remained loyal to the priest and others who were swept off their feet by the inspired Quaker. Margaret Fell became concerned that such a division of opinion should develop in Ulverston during the absence of her husband. She confessed to Mary that "she never had a title in her heart against the truth expressed by George Fox,"[3] but she feared that she would have to make a difficult choice when her husband returned: "I must displease my husband or offend God!" It must have been comforting to Mary to hear another woman express the very sentiments that battled within her own heart.

Three weeks later, at the end of June, Judge Fell returned. As he crossed the sands of the Bay of Lancaster on horseback and neared the shore of the Leven River, he noticed a band of men approaching. They were quick to warn him that his wife and children had been bewitched by a stranger, and that "he must either set them away or all the county would be undone." By the time Judge Fell arrived home, he was in a great state of anxiety. That night George Fox was invited to come in and join the Fell family. After dinner Fox spoke with Margaret's husband and she reported, "If all England had been there, they could not have denied the truth of those things, and so my husband came to see clearly the truth at what he (Fox) spoke, and he was very quiet that night, and said no more and went to bed."[4]

The next day Judge Fell told George Fox that he was welcome to have Quaker meetings at Swarthmore Hall. He apologized to his wife that he felt too old to take on a new religion, much as he admired the Quakers. He never attended the meetings which were held every week at Swarthmore Hall, but he would sit in the study with the door open so that he could hear what they were saying in the next room. As a respected judge, he proved a helpful friend to the Quakers who were often arrested for not observing the customs of the Anglican Church and in need of a legal friend to release them from jail.

Mary Dyer had been at Swarthmore Hall several days before George Fox returned from a mission in the midlands. When he entered the living room, it was as if she had been struck by lightning. Fox was thirty years old, fourteen years younger than Mary. He appeared very neat and fresh for one who had been traveling in the midlands for several weeks. He was dressed in leather breeches and a clean white linen shirt under a doublet, fastened with alchemy buttons. He wore his hair long beneath a broad-brimmed hat. As his piercing eyes met hers, words were not necessary to connect the two.

The next morning Mary Dyer could at last talk with George Fox. Fox recalled his youth in Fenny Drayton in Leicestershire where he had tended sheep for his hard-working parents who were weavers by trade. Working as a cobbler as well as a shepherd, he learned to respect the durable quality of leather as a physical protection against the elements of nature, and he designed and made all his clothes of it.

Fox attended the Presbyterian Church at Fenny Drayton regularly. His father, Christopher Fox, was a respected Church warden and nicknamed "Righteous Criste." George Fox had many questions about religion which he would put to his mother. Her intelligent response made him realize that women sometimes had better answers than men. It was the beginning of his recognition and great respect for women which was to become so influential in the Quaker movement. He became depressed by the long repetitious sermons he heard in church. He wanted a faith to live by and, while tending sheep, he found an entirely different kind of religion. Alone with nature, he experienced a sense of peace he had never felt while listening to haranguing sermons. He was more inspired sitting on the rocks of the fields than on the pews of the Drayton Church. To the great disappointment of his parents, he stopped going to Church with them and instead went off with his Bible into the fields by himself. Gradually, he discovered that the continuity of silence restored his ability to hear. He became convinced that there was a different way to experience the relationship between man and God outside the Church. Depression swung to elation as he began to feel the direct presence of God within himself, and came to realize that the experience he thought was reserved for the apostles was available to every man and woman.

As Fox wandered through the midlands he came to the place where four counties met in the little town of Senbergh, Yorkshire. It was the month of June, time for a big Hiring Fair with people coming from all around to be interviewed and hired for household help. On Sunday, Fox attended the local church which was overcrowded with visitors who seemed to be seeking religious as well as domestic help. After the sermon George Fox got up and spoke and suggested that those who were interested might meet him on Pendle Hill in the afternoon.

Pendle Hill was an outcropping of limestone, one of nature's perfect pulpits. From there one could look over the four adjoining counties and the sea of Lancashire. A thousand people gathered that Sunday afternoon. George Fox looked over the people for a while in silence waiting for a spiritual prompting to speak. Finally he spoke for three hours. His electric voice captivated all those who had gathered there. They had found their apostle.

For four more years George Fox wandered, collecting seekers and preaching in the midlands. The movement was sprouting in many places, but lacked a center. In and out of prison, whipped here and worshipped there, sleeping weeks in haystacks, George Fox continued his mission. In 1652, he arrived in the market town of Ulverston, weather weary and in need of shelter. It was at this time that he heard of the hospitality of Swarthmore Hall, only a mile from Ulverston. His meeting with the Fells had taken place four years before Mary's arrival.

Mary spent the following week in Fox's company, a week pivotal to her life. They walked through the Swarthmore orchards in deep conversation. George Fox convinced her that men and women were equal in God's eyes. Each person had a special inner light to discover. It was Fox's mission to help all people find their own worth and their own capacity for contribution to the world. "God has a mission for every man, woman, and child," he said, "and each person must work to discover his or her own assignment."[5] Mary had never met any man who inspired her so completely, and she began to feel a great change in the way she thought about herself. It was revolutionary for her, as a woman, to be considered equal to any man, and it was the first time she felt that she could completely erase the nagging stigma that she was the "mother of a monster" and therefore a token of the devil.

One day, George Fox took Mary Dyer to visit a school he had started for children. It was a gardening school where children of all ages were planting and tending both flowers and vegetables. Fox explained that by showing children the growth and flowering of seeds, he hoped they might recognize a similar process within them-selves. He also showed them how small plants withered if they were not nurtured. Mary saw that the children were so engrossed in what they were doing they were oblivious to the visitors.

After one of their long conversations, George Fox suggested to Mary Dyer that she become a Quaker minister (or elder, as they were called). This idea was very exciting to Mary, for aside from midwifery, she knew of no profession open to women. The concept that women could be heard in the Quaker religion made it appear like another form of Antinomianism. She could not help but compare them, for she was the only woman to experience both movements. The forms of expression were different. Anne Hutchinson had referred to "salvation by grace," while George Fox referred to "spreading God's seed." The Antinomians belonged to the outward tradition of expressed ideas, in contrast to the shared silence of the individual inner voices of the Quakers.

This quiet union of souls was a new experience for Mary Dyer, and while equality was important to both Antinomians and Quakers, the Quaker movement had raised several issues which epitomized what they meant by equality among men with reverence reserved only for God.

The first was in relation to "Hat Honor." It was the custom of the time to tip one's hat to one's superior. The Quakers would not remove their hats for anyone or anything, except in prayer. God was the only superior who warranted such an act of respect.

Next to Hat Honor was Pronoun Honor. In addressing a superior, the formal "you" was considered more polite than the informal "thee." Quakers decided that the familiar "thee" would be the only pronoun ever used in addressing other people.

The issue which placed the Quakers in the most vulnerable position in society was their refusal to take an oath, for it was the law that every British citizen swear his allegiance to the government. Refusal to do so was punishable by jail. Communities that wanted to repress the Quakers would ask them to swear allegiance, and upon refusal, imprison them. It was an easy way to break up Quaker meetings.

Along with the inspiration of George Fox, Mary would have responded to that beautiful woman, Margaret Fell, as "face answers face in a glass." Eager to share all that she had gathered, Mary would have gone on preaching missions first around the midlands, and then in London where more and more Quaker meetings were beginning to get organized. These Quaker women also served the sick and the poor in London. Mary became an effective preacher. From time to time, she returned to the Quaker base at Swarthmore Hall, a wonderful place for refreshment.

At Swarthmore Hall, Mary met people who became crucial to the rest of her life. One was Edward Burroughs, an ardent nineteen-year-old follower of George Fox. Another, Christopher Holder, was a wealthy young man in his twenties whose dynamic personality and strong feelings gave him the confidence to conquer the world. Marmaduke Stevenson was a farmer from Yorkshire. While plowing his field the Lord told him to put down his plow, leave his family, and follow the calling. Then there was Mary Fisher, who had been in jail for two years, and Ann Austin, the mother of five children. Mary Dyer was the only one who had lived in America. No one else from Swarthmore Hall had crossed the ocean, but there were plenty getting ready to go.

George Fox wanted to spread the Quaker movement as far as possible, and missionaries went to Ireland, Wales, and Scotland, as well as the far reaches of England. By 1655, Fox decided the time had come to extend the mission across the Atlantic. Women were the first volunteers. Never before had they been given the opportunity to carry out such a venture on their own.

The earliest overseas Quaker stronghold was established in the British West Indies. Favored as it was by the prevailing Atlantic winds and currents, Barbados became a convenient stopover between England and the American mainland. The island was treasured for its sumptuous supply of sugar cane. Lieut. Col. Rous was a wealthy sugar planter already established in Barbados. His son, John Rous, became an important Quaker convert who eventually married one of the Fells' daughters. One of the Swarthmore Hall collection of letters is from John Rous to Margaret Fells reporting on Mary Dyer's visit to Barbados, which was becoming known as "The Nursery of the Truth." Once Mary left that "Nursery", she was never again to enjoy the peace of her new Quaker religion without disturbance.

*****

Judge Fell died in 1653 and Margaret Fell married George Fox in 1669.

16. Swarthmore Hall
(unknown English engraver--courtesy of Swarthmore College).

17. Portrait of George Fox (by unknown English
engraver--courtesy of Haverford College).

18. Portrait of John Endicott (by John Smibert--
courtesy of the Massachusetts Historical Society).

{ 18 }
Mary's Return

John Endicott, who had succeeded John Winthrop in 1649, remained Governor of Massachusetts Bay Colony, excepting two years as deputy, until his death in 1665. His government was more vulnerable to the Quaker beliefs than any other in the New World, for everything the colony stood for was directly opposed to the Quaker ideals, and found them threatening. Endicott had a volatile disposition, often facing difficult problems with displays of rage. He once had cut out the cross in the middle of the British flag to assert the separation of the Church of Salem from the Church of England. For this deed he was excluded from public office for one whole year. Army-trained, he commanded the Boston troops sent to fight the Pequot Indians, and he demonstrated his ruthlessness by extensive burning of Indian property as well as slaying every Pequot man, woman and child in sight, bringing their severed limbs back to Boston as a proud testament to his military victory. He was a far more intolerant man than John Winthrop.

Although the conflict between Quakers and Puritans was over religious matters, the result was political. The Quakers maintained that God created all men and women equal, while the Puritans preached that God's ultimate design was a hierarchy. While Quakers turned to the "inner light" as a source of "truth," the Puritans believed such revelations blasphemous, asserting that the Bible was the only guide to all life. Governor Endicott feared that, if he permitted the Quakers to express their views in Massachusetts Bay Colony, the whole structure of the Church-State partnership might collapse; and England would take over.

Mary Fisher and Ann Austin were the first Quakers to arrive in

Boston. No sooner did they disembark than they were led to the Boston jail for three weeks before being sent back.

On August 9, 1656, a small craft from England called Speedwell entered Boston Harbor. The port authorities were alerted to search the boat before anyone landed. The passenger list had "Q's" beside the names of four men and four women, indicating that they were Quakers. Endicott ordered that these eight should be brought directly to the Boston court. Christopher Holder and John Copeland led the group, marching past a jeering crowd to the Massachusetts General Court. Endicott had summoned some local ministers to help him examine these Quakers, but Christopher Holder and John Copeland responded readily to their questions and dumbfounded the authorities by their familiarity with the Bible. Even more irritating to Governor Endicott than Christopher Holder's familiarity with the Bible was his knowledge of the law. When they were marched back to jail, Christopher Holder and John Copeland made immediate demands for their release, claiming that there was no law that justified their imprisonment.

Governor Endicott knew this was true. There was nothing in the Massachusetts Bay Colony Charter which permitted the imprisonment of anyone merely on grounds of their religious belief. He felt very threatened by the sophistication as well as the fervor of this young man, Christopher Holder. And so he devised a tactic to get rid of the Quakers. The General Court that met in Boston in mid-October of 1656, 1657, and 1658 passed anti-Quaker laws of increasing severity. They failed to realize that the toughening of the laws only served to strengthen the wills of their opponents.

On October 14, 1656, the Court ordered:

That what master or commander of any ship, barke, pinnace, catch, or any other vessel that shall henceforth bring into any harbor, creeks, or cove without jurisdiction any known Quaker or Quakers, or any other blasphemous heretics shall pay ... the fine of 100 pounds... [and] they must be brought back from where they came or go to prison.

After trying to cover all the loopholes in any possible entry to Boston, the Massachusetts Court addressed what it would do with anyone who persisted successfully. It was decided that such a person should go to the House of Correction and be severely whipped, kept constantly at work, and not allowed to speak to anyone. They set up certain fines: 54 pounds for having any Quaker books or writing "concerning their devilish opinions," 40 pounds for defending any Quaker or their books, 44 pounds for a second offence, and the "House of Correction for a third offence ... until there be a convenient passage for them to be sent out of this land." Anyone who spoke against the magistrates would be whipped and fined 54 pounds. These laws were read on the street corners of Boston, with the beat of drums for emphasis.

As Christopher Holder and John Copeland sat in their cells in the Boston jail, they could hear the rattling of drums and the calling out of the newly-written laws. They realized that they were going to have to leave on the next available ship departing for England.

Mary Dyer and Anne Burden were on the third ship to arrive. After a stormy crossing, stopping first at Barbados, they landed in Boston in January/February 1657. Anne Burden was returning to Boston after her husband's death to settle his estate. Mary Dyer was coming back to join her family in Newport after seven years in England. Not aware of the first anti-Quaker law, they anticipated a happy landing in Boston after their rough winter voyage. To their utter dismay, both women were jailed as soon as they arrived. For two and a half months they remained incommunicado in their darkened cells with boarded up windows. Mary's books and Quaker papers were all burned by the jail warden, who was also bribed by an elderly man, Nicholas Upsall, to bring her food. Although Mary Dyer had visited prisons in England, she had never known such darkness, dampness, and chill. The English dungeons were dreadful, but the prisoners were allowed to walk in the castle grounds from time to time. Every night, as Mary lay on the prickly straw bedding, she wondered how she was going to get word to William of her whereabouts. She was finally able to slip a letter out through a crack to someone outside the jail. It took a long time for the letter to reach

William Dyer in Newport.

* * * *

Governor Endicott was startled when William Dyer walked into his home demanding that his wife should be freed immediately. John Endicott knew that although Boston had disenfranchised William Dyer, he was highly respected by the Boston authorities for his prominent position in Rhode Island. Endicott did not want to jeopardize his relationship with the neighboring colony. They would have to free Mary Dyer because of the prestige of her husband, but only on a condition. William Dyer was put under a heavy bond and made to "give his honor" that if his wife was allowed to return home, he was "not to lodge her in any town of the colony nor to permit any to have speech with her on the journey." Under no conditions should Mary Dyer ever return to Massachusetts. When William Dyer reluctantly agreed to these terms, he was escorted to the Boston jail to release his wife. It was not the kind of homecoming that Mary or William had looked forward to.

How galling for Mary to be silenced like a misbehaving child as she returned to her home. Seven years had transformed the Newport she remembered. The woods had been thinned to accommodate a forest of masts now decorating the harbor. Houses, piers, people, cattle, everything seemed to have multiplied.

The most spectacular growth was on Dyer Farm, where seven years had changed dramatically the appearance of each of the Dyer children. Samuel was now twenty-two with a wife called Anne, the daughter of Captain Edward Hutchinson and granddaughter of the blessed Anne. Little Mary, at seventeen, had become the mistress of the household. Will was sixteen, Maher eleven, Henry nine, and Charles seven years old. Mary had been so long away she felt more like a visiting aunt than a mother. As each child gradually referred to her as "Mother," that awkward feeling of being a visitor in her home began to diminish.

How strange it must have felt to witness the presence of her own six children, seven years later, searching her memory for distant recollections to help her identify these little strangers. She must have yearned to dissolve the guilt of absentee parenthood. And yet, beneath the sincere desire to reconstruct her role as wife and mother, ever emerging was that frightening fraction of a wish that her family would somehow disappear and leave her alone with her mission. She knew that she could depend on a most remarkable husband, who not only had brought up their family as a single parent, but had also served the Colony in very important roles. Mary had reversed the sexual responsibilities in a manner unheard of for her times — and yet William had not faltered in his love and respect for her. Their marriage might be considered unusual today, but three hundred and forty years ago, it was utterly unique.

As Mary reviewed her family, it was clear that only William had remained the same size, with the same voice and expression. Mary called him, "thee," but his response to her was "you." Neither would change. Would this new combination of "thee" and "you" ever again feel   like   "we"?

{ 19 }
Christopher Holder

M ary Dyer could not forget her experience in the Boston jail.
She kept wondering what had happened to the others who
had been jailed on their arrival in Boston. The passengers
of the *Swallow* and the *Speedwell* had all been forced to
sail away from Boston. Where were they? Barbados? England? She
longed for news of her fellow Quakers.

Mary did not know that the captain of the *Speedwell* had returned
Christopher Holder and the seven other banished passengers to the
shores of England. Once landed, Christopher wasted no time in
getting in touch with George Fox. He wanted to take the first possible
ship back to America. The expense was no problem. He had the
money to finance a whole Quaker expedition. His interest was in
finding a ship. George Fox got in touch with Robert Fowler, who had
just completed the building of a small barque called *Woodhouse*.

George Fox felt moved to write a letter for Christopher Holder to
deliver to his "friends across the sea that have Blacks and Indians as
Slaves" reminding them of the word of the Gospel that "every
captured creature under the whole Heaven" deserves liberty and
freedom.

Seventeen Friends signed up for the trip. John Copeland was the
first. Sarah Gibbons, Mary Weatherhead, and Dorothy Waugh, the
three women who had been on the round trip of the *Speedwell*, all
signed up for their third ocean voyage within one year, broken only
by the weeks spent in the Boston jail. They were joined by Mary
Clark, Richard Doudney, William Brend, Humphrey Norton, and
William Robinson. None of the passengers or crew had any
knowledge of navigation. They embarked without a compass,
planning to sail west in a straight line for 3,000 miles. Robert Fowler

wrote in the Woodhouse log about the voyage as "performed by the Lord as he did Noah's Ark, where he shut up a few righteous persons and landed them safely even on Mt. Ararat."[1] Later, he wrote, "We saw the Lord leading our vessel as if it were a man leading a horse by the head; we regarding [n]either latitude or longitude." Miraculously, the "horse" came galloping through the hellgate passage and landed in the Dutch plantation of New Amsterdam Harbor in less than two months!

After they disembarked in New Amsterdam, William Robinson and most of the other *Woodhouse* passengers headed south on a mission to Maryland and Virginia. Christopher Holder and John Copeland had their hearts set on returning to Massachusetts. They sailed the *Woodhouse* up Narragansett Bay, landing in Providence.

Once in Providence, Christopher Holder tried to deliver the message from George Fox to Roger Williams, but Roger was not interested. Although he, like Mary Dyer, had left the Anabaptist Church to become a Seeker, he had no intention of joining the Quakers, protesting that, "They admit no interpreter but themselves, for the spirit within, they say, gave forth the Scripture, and is above the Scripture, ... and that all they do and say is scripture " Papists and Quakers most horribly and hypocritically trample it under their proud feet."

For the rest of his life, Roger Williams carried on a transatlantic exchange of arguments with George Fox, whom he described as running "round again and again like the windmill sails." That he could still tolerate those with whom he fiercely disagreed was one of the great qualities of Roger Williams.

When the news reached Newport that a ship called *Woodhouse* had arrived in Providence carrying Quakers, Mary Dyer hurried to catch a ferry. She went directly to the home of her good friends, the Scotts. Catherine Scott was a sister of Anne Hutchinson, and she and her husband, Richard, were already active Quakers. As Mary entered the Scott's home she was startled to see the handsome young man she had been so attracted to at Morecomb Bay. Christopher Holder had left the Boston jail and departed from the city just before her arrival. She listened to the story of the Quakers sailing across the ocean without a compass. It was a miracle to take to heart. A fearless loyalty and determination between all those involved in the Quaker faith was begun at this meeting at the Scotts in Providence. For the Scotts, it was a total family affair. Their daughters, Mary and Patience, were eager participants. Mary Dyer noticed that Christopher Holder was immediately attracted to Mary Scott. He kept looking at her and edging across the room to be close to her.

After the gathering of Quakers at the Scott household, Mary Dyer boarded the *Woodhouse* to sail back to Newport with Christopher Holder and John Copeland. Christopher was determined to return to Boston as soon as possible to challenge Governor Endicott and the magistrates.

The Woodhouse sailed to the windward of Prudence Island, reaching for Dyer Island, where William's hogs were grunting and slurping over clams by the edge of the shore. Slipping down the coast, they could see the Dyer Farm set just behind Coaster Island. Past Rose, and Goat Islands, they entered Newport Harbor.

Christopher Holder and John Copeland agreed to stay with the Dyers until they could figure out a way of getting to Boston. They knew it would be foolhardy to try and sail the *Woodhouse* there, being all too familiar with the law of 1656 preventing ships with Quakers on board from landing. But they were determined to pursue their mission to spread the Quaker message throughout Massachusetts Bay Colony. They would have to find another way of entering. After several days of exploring different possibilities they located a fishing boat in Providence which volunteered to drop them off at Martha's Vineyard.

In the meantime, Mary Dyer had become interested in the activities of three other shipmates of Christopher Holder's on the Woodhouse. Humphrey Norton had been arrested in New Haven and held for three weeks in prison, where he was very maltreated. William Brend and Mary Weatherhead joined Mary Dyer in her plan to "enter" New Haven and pursue their Quaker mission. They arrived to find anti-Quaker laws[2] in action. Mary was arrested and "set on a horse" and ordered to leave. As she galloped away she was heard to cry out, "Wo be unto you, for Humphrey Norton's sake: Wo be unto you for the cruelty done to him!"[3]

While Mary Dyer was being rebuked in New Haven, Christopher Holder and John Copeland were being ordered to leave Martha's Vineyard. Hiding in the sand dunes for several days, they met up with friendly Indians who volunteered to help them cross over to Massachusetts. The Indians paddled them to Cape Cod, and directed them across the sand dunes and through the pine woods to Sandwich, where they found a community of people unsettled in their religious affiliations. Christopher Holder and John Copeland arrived at the perfect moment, for the people of Sandwich had just lost their minister and were in need of religious leadership. Holder and Copeland were received with enthusiasm by about eighteen families who were ready to become Quakers. Finding a lovely dell by a quiet stream in the woods, they called their enchanted hideaway "Christopher's Hollow," a name which has remained with the place. A circle of Friends gathered together and sat on a circle of stones to share their religious convictions. It was the first real Friends meeting in America, and the start of regular meetings.

Happy with this success, Christopher Holder and John Copeland moved on to conquer other communities. From Sandwich, they went to Duxbury, and then from town to town in Massachusetts, leaving fifteen converted Quaker "ministers" in their wake. Eventually, Governor Endicott got wind of their activities and alerted scouts throughout New England to arrest them, but John Copeland and Christopher Holder remained free until they walked into Salem.

John Endicott had founded Salem and it was his home. When Holder arrived at the Salem Congregational Church, he listened to the sermon of the day, and then, in his usual manner, he arose in the rear of the church to challenge what had been said and present the Quaker alternatives.[4] One of Endicott's army was standing ready. He seized Holder, hurled him bodily to the floor of the church and stuffed a leather glove and handkerchief down his throat. Holder turned blue, gagged, and gasped for life. He was close to death when a member of the congregation sprang to the rescue. Samuel Shattuck pushed Endicott's envoy aside and retrieved the glove and handkerchief from Holder's throat, and then worked hard to resuscitate him. A lifelong friendship between Samuel Shattuck and Christopher Holder started at that moment.

Holder, Copeland, and Shattuck were all taken to the Boston prison, where Shattuck was freed by paying a 20 shilling bond. Holder and Copeland were brought before Endicott. He ordered that they should each have thirty lashes. They returned black and bleeding to jail, where they spent three days without food or bedding.

The Boston General Court met again in mid-October, 1657. The original anti-Quaker law had not taken care of the problems. The Boston magistrates would have to strengthen their authority. After much discussion, they passed a second anti-Quaker law, which ordered that anyone in the jurisdiction who helped a Quaker to enter the Colony should pay 110 shillings fine and go to prison, and anyone who entertained a Quaker be fined 40 shillings for every hour. The Boston magistrates also tried to decide on a punishment tough enough to scare away the Quakers themselves. They finally decided that any banished Quaker who returned to Massachusetts Bay Colony should suffer as follows:

> Every such male Quaker shall for the first offense have one of his ears cut off and be kept at work in the House of Correction until he can be sent away at his own charge; and for the second offense he shall have his other ear cut off. Every woman Quaker ... shall be severely whipped ... and sent to the House of Correction.

The same punishment would be administered for a woman's second offense. But for a third offense,

> Every Quaker, he or she, ... shall have their tongues bored through with a hot iron ... and kept at the House of Correction.

In the meantime, Christopher Holder was writing a different kind of document in the Boston prison. He had successfully hidden one horn of ink for the purpose. Joined by their Woodhouse mate, Richard Doudney, who had been arrested in Dedham, Holder and Copeland wrote the first Quaker Declaration of Faith:

Whereas, it is reported by them that have not a bridle to their tongues, that we, who are by the world called Quakers, are blasphemous, heretics, and deceivers; therefore we who are here in prison, shall in a few words, declare unto all people that may see this the ground of our religion, and the faith that we contend for, and the cause whereof we suffer.

As [for us] we do believe in the only true and living God, the Father of our Lord Jesus Christ, who have made the heavens and earth, the sea and all things in them contained, and doth uphold all things that he hath created by the word of his power, who at sundry times and in divers manners, spake in times past to our fathers, by the prophets, but in these last days he hath spoken unto us, by his Son, whom he hath made heir of all things, by whom he made the world.

Therefore, while you have light, believe in the light, that ye may be children of the light...

October 1657, House of Correction

    Christopher Holder   John Copeland

        Richard Doudney

The Declaration was written under great suffering. Every week, Holder, Copeland and Doudney were beaten. After two and a half months, they were released, but were soon to return.

On April 15, 1658, Holder and Copeland came back to Cape Cod to reunite with their first circle of Friends in Sandwich. The circumference had grown, spreading out over Christopher's Hollow in joyous reunion. It was there that Christopher met Nicholas Davis, a merchant of Hyannis with a warehouse on Lewis Bay.

The woods surrounding Christopher's Hollow did not serve as sufficient protection for the second meeting of the Sandwich Friends, for Governor Endicott's spies arrested Holder and Copeland in the middle of their meeting and marched them to Barnstable. They were followed by a sober line of people who walked behind "to cheer their brethren in bonds." When they reached Barnstable, Holder and Copeland were stripped and bound to the post of an outhouse. With the standard three-corded rope, they were each given 33 lashes, until their bodies ran with blood. The people of Sandwich stood in horror as "ear and eye witnesses to the cruelty."[5]

After Christopher Holder recovered from the Barnstable scourging, he learned that there were no more Friends to challenge Endicott's anti-Quaker policy in Boston and that Mary Dyer had already been banished from New Haven for her Quaker preaching. She was recovering at home from a bout of pneumonia. Holder located his friend Copeland and they returned to Boston on June 3, 1658. They were arrested in Dedham and once more brought to the Massachusetts Court.

Christopher Holder, more than any other Quaker, was the prime provoker of the Boston magistrates. They feared his charisma, his aristocratic background, his fearlessness and his knowledge. When Governor Endicott recognized Holder and Copeland and realized that the two men who had so frequently defied him had returned, he was in a rage.

"You shall have your ears cut off," he snarled. Puzzled, he inquired, "What, you remain in the same opinion as before?"

Holder answered, "We remain in the fear of the Lord."

Endicott questioned, "The Lord commanded you to come? Nay, it was Satan!" Endicott then turned to Ed Rawson with a directive to be sent to the Keeper of the House of Correction:

> You are ... required to take into your custody the bodies of Christopher Holder and John Copeland and then safely to keep them close at work, with prisoners diet only, till their ears be cut off; and not suffer them any converse with any, while they are in your custody.

John Rous II, from Barbados, was soon to join Holder and Copeland in the House of Correction. On July 7, 1658, those three Friends were brought in for questioning at the Court of Assistants. The sentence they received was originally devised by the Star Chamber in England in 1634 to punish the Puritans William Prynne, Henry Burton, and Dr. Bostwick.

The sentencing of Christopher Holder, John Copeland, and John Rous created a great stir in Boston.[6] Friends poured out of Rhode Island towards Boston in protest. Endicott was disturbed by this public reaction. As a result, he broke the English rule and ordered the slicing of ears done in private. When the prisoners heard of this break with English tradition, they wrote Cromwell in protest.

On July 17, 1658, Holder, Copeland, and Rous were brought into a private prison cell for the operation. John Rous turned to Captain James Oliver and said, "We have appealed to the Chief Magistrate of England. Such execution as this should be done publicly but not in private, for this was contrary to Law of England."

Captain James Oliver snapped, "We do it in private to keep you from talking."

The warden pulled back Holder's hair and then turned his back as he raised his knife.

John Rous protested, saying, "Turn about and see it, for so were his orders."

The marshall was filled with dread and cried out, "Yet, let us look at it."

Christopher Holder, John Copeland, and John Rous were so stalwart while their ears were removed, that the persecutors began to feel that this was insufficient punishment. Therefore, the three one-eared men were whipped after the operation and beaten twice a week for the next nine weeks. The public protest against the treatment of Holder, Copeland and Rous, aroused the anger of the Boston magistrates even more. The Boston jail was full of Christopher's "callers." Reverend Norton declared, "I would carry fire in one hand and faggots in the other to burn all the Quakers in the world."

Mary Dyer had recovered from her pneumonia and was visiting the Scotts in Providence when the word came of Christopher Holder's treatment. Mary Scott was particularly upset that the man she planned to marry was suffering so much. Catherine, her mother, and Patience, her eleven-year-old sister, volunteered to accompany her to Boston to protest. Mary Dyer and another Quaker friend, Hope Clifton, also decided to go. In their eagerness, they walked the whole way from Providence to Boston.

Mary went because she could not stay away from those suffering prisoners. She was susceptible to the high spirits of young men like Christopher Holder, Harry Vane, and George Fox; in their ardor they seemed closer to God than did her even, constant, practical husband. William could not understand her behavior, but his love for her did not change.

All five women were taken to jail as soon as they arrived in Boston. People were pouring in from Newport as well as Providence. Among the other recently-arrived protestors in the Boston jail were William Robinson and Marmaduke Stevenson. It did not take long for the word to get back to Newport that Mary Dyer was among those in jail.

{ 20 }
Pain of Death

The decision which shattered the world was made at the second session of the General Court in Boston on October 19, 1658. The vote was 12 to 11, with one absent member, and it was not taken without conflict. The missing magistrate, who was home sick, said he would have crawled on his knees to oppose the law. He begged for a re-balloting, but he was refused. The law was passed and read:

> Whereas there is a pernitious sect, commonly called Quakers, lately risen, who by word and writing have published and maintayned many dangerous and harid tennetts, and do take upon them to change and alter the received laudable customes of our nation in giving civill respect to aequalls or reverence to superiors, whose actions tend to undermine the authority of civil government, as also to destroy the order of the churches by denying all established forms of worship, and by withdrawing from the order church assemblies ... and frequenting private meetings of their own ...
>
> For prevention every Quaker who is not an inhabitant but found within the jurisdiction ... shall be committed to prison until the next Court of Assistant meets where they will be tried and if they are convicted of being the Quaker sect shall be sentenced to BANISHMENT UPON PAIN OF DEATH.[1]

During the next session of the Court of Assistants, Mary Dyer, William Robinson, Marmaduke Stevenson, and Nicholas Davis were sent for. All four were sentenced to "banishment on pain of death" under the new law.

Nicholas Davis had been recognized as a member of the Sandwich Circle of Friends when he was at the Boston port arranging to ship some barrels of his pickled oysters to Barbados. After his sentence he hastily returned to his warehouse on Lewis Bay on Cape Cod and arranged for future exports to leave from the port of Hyannis and he eventually moved with his barque Trysall to the free town of Newport.

William Robinson and Marmaduke Stevenson left Boston, but not the Massachusetts Bay Colony. In Salem, they found some "ready followers" with whom they could continue their Quaker teaching. The group had several good meetings in the outlying woods of Salem before Governor Endicott's scouts apprehended them and led Robinson and Stevenson right back to the Boston jail.

In the meantime, Mary Dyer had returned to her home in Newport after the sentence of "banishment on pain of death." When news reached her that William Robinson and Marmaduke Stevenson were back in the Boston jail, there was no way that she could remain at home. She felt "called upon" to visit her Quaker friends in the Boston jail. They must be supported and encouraged in their Quaker mission. By now, Mary was familiar with the Indian trails which wound through the woods between Mount Hope and Boston. She knew how to obtain a horse and where to change horses if necessary.

While Mary Dyer was ferrying across Mount Hope Bay and searching out the paths through the woods towards Boston, Christopher Holder was making his plans to return to England and to seek counsel with George Fox and Edward Burroughs. By the time Mary arrived in Boston, Christopher was already making inquiries about the next departing ship. As both Christopher and Mary were intent on visiting their friends, William Robinson and Marmaduke Stevenson, it was not surprising that they ran into one another outside the jail. They met as two friends sharing a mission which defied all other considerations.[2] Although they were both aware that they had been "banished on pain of death," they fell into a deep conversation right in front of the Boston jail. Conspicuous, vulnerable, and unretractable, they conversed with spiritual ecstasy, remaining aloof to danger until they were dragged into the jail, not as visitors, but prisoners.

The Boston magistrates were exasperated to exhaustion by this transgression. They feared repercussions from England because of Christopher Holder's highborn background. The Massachusetts Bay Charter was already at risk. As long as Christopher was making his own plans to return to England, the magistrates decided that it would be preferable to insist on his departure instead of a hanging.[3]

Thus, Christopher approached the brink of disaster and then, at the last minute, escaped to safety ... while others suffered the final penalty.

19. William's second letter (see page 184) to the Boston
magistrates (courtesy of Harriet Dyer Reed).

{ 21 }
A Husband's Plea

In 1657, when William Dyer rescued Mary from the Boston jail, he had given his word of honor to Governor Endicott that his wife would stay out of Massachusetts. In 1658, she had slipped back to Boston to visit Christopher Holder in prison and now, a year later, she was paying calls on William Robinson and Marmaduke Stevenson in the same jail. Instead of going to Boston to rescue his unpredictable wife on August 30, 1659, William Dyer sat down at his desk to write a long and urgent letter to the Court of Assistants which was scheduled to assemble in Boston on September 6.

Gentlemen:

Having received some letters from my wife, I am given to understand of the commitment to close prison to a place (according to description) not unlike Bishop Bonner's rooms ... It is a sad condition, in executing such cruelties towards their fellow creatures and sufferers ... Had you no commiseration of a tender soul that being wett to the skin, you cause her to thrust into a room whereon was nothing to sitt or lye down upon but dust ... had your dogg been wett you would have offered it the liberty of a chimney corner to dry itself, or had your hoggs been pend in a sty, you would have offered them some dry straw, or else you would have wanted mercy to your beast, but alas Christians now with you are used worse [than] hoggs or doggs ... oh merciless cruelties.

William Dyer reminded the Boston magistrates that they had no evidence against his wife and, therefore, no legal right to imprison her.

> You have done more in persecution in one year than the worst bishops did in seven, and now to add more towards a tender woman ... that gave you no just cause against her for did she come to your meeting to disturb them as you call itt, or did she come to reprehend the magistrates' [She] only came to visit her friends in prison and when dispatching that her intent of returning to her family as she declared in her (statement) the next day to the Governor, therefore it is you that disturbed her, else why was she not let alone. [What] house entered she to molest or what did she, that like a malefactor she must be hauled to [prison] or what law did she transgress? She was about a business justifiable before God and all good men"

The worst of men, the bishops themselves, denied not the visitation and release of friends to their prisoners, which myself hath often experienced by visiting Mr. Prine, Mr. Smart and other eminent [men] yea when he was commanded close in the towne, I had resort once or twice a week and [I was] never fetched before authority to ask me wherefore I came to the towne, or Kings bench, or Gatehouse ... had there not been more adventurous tender hearted professors than yo'selves many of them you call godly ministers and others might have perished ... if that course you take had been in use with them, as to send for a person and ask them whe'fore they came thither. What hath not people in America the same liberty as beasts and birds to pass the land or air without examination?

Have you a law that says the light in M. Dyre is not M. Dyre's rule, if you have for that or any the fornamed a law, she may be made a transgresso', for words and your mittimus hold good, but if not, then have you imprisoned her and punisht her without law and against the Law of god and man ... behold my wife without law and against Law is imprison' and punished and so higly punisht as intended to stepp next into death ... she is condemned for saying the light is the Rule! It is not your light within your rule by which you make and act such lawes for ye have no rule of Gods word in the Bible to make a law titled Quakers nor have you any order from the Supreme State of England to make such lawes. Therefore, it must be your light within you is your rule and you walk by ... Remember what Jesus Christ said, "if the light that be in you is darkness, how great is that darkness".

... conscience, the first and next words after appearance is "You are a Quaker" see the steppes you follow and let their misery be your warning; and then if answer be not made according to the ruling will; away with them to the Cobhole or new Prison, or House of Correction ... And now Gentlemen consider their ends, and believe it, itt was certaine the Bishops ruine suddenly followed after their hott persuanes of some godly people by them called Puritans ... especially when they proceeded to suck the blood of Mr. Prine, Mr. Burton, and Dr. Bostwicks eares, only them three and butt three, and they were as odious to them as the Quakers are to you.

In a final enclave of arguments designed to demonstrate the multitude of their illegalities, William Dyer demanded,

What witness or legal testimony was taken that my wife Mary Dyre was a Quaker, if not before God and man how can you clear yourselves and seat of justice, from cruelty persecution ye as so fair as in you lies murder as to her and to myself and family oppression and tiranny. The God of truth knows all this. This is the sum and totals of a law titled Quakers: that she is guilty of a breach of a tittled Quakers is as strange, that she is lawfully convicted of 2 witnesses is not heard of, that she must be banished by a law tittled Quakers being not convicted by law but considered by surmise and condemned to close prison by Mr. Bellingham"s suggestion is so absurd and ridiculous, the meanest pupil in law will hiss at such proceeds in Old Lawyers ... is your law tittled Quakers Felony or Treason, that vehement suspicion render them capable of suffering ... If you be men I suppose your fundamental lawes is that noe person shall be imprisoned or molested but upon the breach of a law, yett behold my wife without law and against law is imprisoned and punished.

My wife writes me word and information, ye she had been above a fortnight and had not trode on the ground, but saw it out your window; what inhumanity is this, had you never wives of your own, or ever any tender affection to a woman, deal so with a woman, what has nature forgotten if refreshment be debarred?

I have written thus plainly to you, being exceedingly sensible of the unjust molestations and detaining of my deare yokefellow, mine and my familyes want of her will crye loud in yo' eares together with her sufferings of your part but I questions not mercy favor and comfort from the most high of her owne soule, that at present my self and family bea by you deprived of the comfort and refreshment we might have enjoyed by her [presence].

her husband,
W. Dyre
Newport this 30 August 1659

William slowly shook sand over the wet words before replacing his quill in the ink horn. He felt as if he had written all he could. The strips of script formed a tidy horizontal design which did not indicate the turbulence of the contents. Only the signature suggested the flamboyance of William Dyer — the letters like dogs' ears in the wind. William had been in such total concentration over his letter since early dawn that he was surprised to look out and see the afternoon shadows creeping across the yard. He must hasten to find an Indian messenger to run with it to Boston.[2]

20. Mary Dyer confronting Boston's magistrates (by Edwin Austin Abby--courtesy of Social Law Library, Boston).

{ 22 }
Letters From Mary

Just before Christopher Holder left for England, the Massachusetts General Court met on October 20, 1659. Mary Dyer, William Robinson, and Marmaduke Stevenson had orders to appear. Governor Endicott was exasperated. He would have given anything to be rid of the annoying Quakers. Like a frenzied parent, ```tried by a misbehaving child, he had stretched the threatened punishment beyond any anticipation of its use. "I'll kill you if you don't stop bothering me." The pressure was mounting and now he was faced with the horrible reality of taking action to prove his point. He was frightened of his own power — the decision to kill.

When Mary Dyer, William Robinson, and Marmaduke Stevenson were brought before the Council of State for questioning, Endicott was trembling.[1] He spoke in a faint voice and was described as appearing "as a man out of dust whose life had departed." First, he ordered the men to remove their hats. Then in a shaky voice which could hardly be heard, he said, "We have tried several laws and endeavored in several ways to keep you from amongst us, and neither whippings, nor imprisoning, nor cutting of ears, nor banishing you upon pain of death would keep you from amongst us..." His voice became even fainter, the whisper was hardly audible when he announced, "Give ear and hearken now to your sentence of death."

Governor Endicott first addressed William Robinson and Marmaduke Stevenson, who were both hastily dispatched to prison with the verdict, "You shall be had to the place from which you came, and from thence to the gallows and there to be hanged until you are dead."

Mary Dyer was left standing alone in the courtroom, when Governor Endicott repeated the same verdict to her.

She closed her eyes and smiled beautifully, saying "The will of the Lord be done."

Endicott was unnerved by her composure, and shouted, "Take her away, Marshall!"

Mary responded, "Yea, joyfully I go."

As the Marshall led her from the General Court down Main Street, on their way back to the House of Correction, she turned to him and said, "I shall go to the prison without you. Let me alone." The Marshall replied respectfully, "I believe you, Mrs. Dyer, but I must do what I am commanded."

That week in jail, Mary Dyer, William Robinson, and Marmaduke Stevenson sat in their cells writing their last pleas to the General Court to change the laws of banishment upon pain of death.

Mary Dyer wrote two letters to the Massachusetts General Court, the only documents we have written by her. She wrote these letters under the most difficult circumstances in a damp, chilly cell with hardly a ray of light, her forbidden writing materials hidden under her skirt or straw mattress.

The earlier descriptions of Mary Dyer come to life in these letters, as "a person of no mean extract and parentage, a comely stature and countenance, of a piercing knowledge in many things, of a wonderful sweet and pleasant discourse, so fit for great affairs that she wanted nothing manly, except only the name and sex."

She addressed Governor Endicott and the Boston magistrates as a woman confident of her own charm, knowledge, and purpose. Referring to the Old Testament, the basis of their laws, she chose King Ahasuerus as a model for Governor Endicott and Esther as the role model for herself. Esther seduced the King to release the Jews. Endicott could become a similar hero by following the advice of Mary to change the laws and free the Quakers.

After her reference to King Ahasuerus and Esther, Mary switched roles and became the Quaker missionary, instructing the Boston magistrates that they also had "God's seed" within them. Salvation depended on their recognition of their own inner light. She recommended that they read the Proverbs to pick up some of the messages they had missed. After a series of gentle suggestions, Mary wound up with full power, "God will not be mocked!"

The Boston magistrates could not hear the message; they were too frightened of losing their identity as leaders of God's unique community. If they had taken Mary's advice and changed their laws of persecution, they might have regained respect and survived. Instead, they continued to play a losing game.

Mary Dyer's first letter read:

Whereas I am by many charged with the Guiltiness of my own Blood: if you mean in my Coming to Boston, I am therein clear, and justified by the Lord, in whose Will I came, who will require my Blood of you, be sure, who have made a Law to take away the Lives of the Innocent Servants of God, if they come among you, who are called by you, "Cursed Quakers," altho I say, and am a Living Witness for them and the Lord, that he hath blessed them, and sent them unto you: Therefore, be not found Fighters against God, but let my Counsel and Request be accepted with you, To repeal all such Laws, that the Truth and Servants of the Lord, may have free Passage among you and you be kept from shedding innocent Blood, which I know there are many among you would not do, if they knew it so to be: Nor can the Enemy that stirreth you up thus to destroy this holy Seed, in any Measure countervail, the great Damage that you will by thus doing procure: Therefore, seeing the Lord hath not hid it from me, it lyeth upon me, in Love to your Souls, thus to persuade you: I have no Self Ends, the Lord knoweth, for if my Life were freely granted by you, it would not avail me, nor could I expect it of you, so long as I shall daily hear or see, of the Sufferings of these People, my dear Brethren and Seed, with whom my Life is bound up, as I have done these two Years, and not it is like to increase, even unto Death, for no evil Doing, but Coming among you: Was ever the like laws heard of, among a People that profess Christ come in the Flesh? And have such no other Weapons, but such Laws, to fight with against spiritual Wickedness with all, as you call it? Wo is me for you! Of whom take you Counsel! Search with the light of Christ in you, and it will show you of whom, as it hath done me, and many more, who have been disobedient and deceived, as now you are, which Light, as you come into, and obey what is made manifest to you therein, you will not repent, that you were kept from shedding Blood, tho be a Woman: It's not my own Life I seek (for I chose rather to suffer with the People of God, than to enjoy the Pleasures of Egypt) but the Life of the Seed, which I know the Lord hath blessed, and therefore seeks the Enemy thus vehemently the Life thereof to destroy, as in all ages he ever did: Oh! hearken not unto him, I beseech you, for the Seed's Sake, which is One in all, and is dear in the Sight of God; which they that touch, Touch the Apple of his Eye, and cannot escape his Wrath; whereof I having felt, cannot but persuade all Men that I have to do withal, especially you who name the Name of Christ, to depart from such Iniquity, as SHEDDING BLOOD, EVEN OF THE SAINTS OF THE Most High. Therefore let my Request have as much Acceptance with you, if you be Christians as Esther had with Ahasuerus whose relation is short of that that's between Christians and my Request is the same that her's was: and he said not, that he had made a Law, and it would be dishonourable for him to revoke it: but when he understood that these People were so prized by her, and so nearly concerned her (as in Truth these are to me) as you may see what he did for her: Therefore I leave these Lines with you, appealing to the faithful and true Witness of God, which is One in all Consciences, before whom we must all appear; with whom I shall eternally rest, in Everlasting Joy and Peace, whether you will hear or forebear: With him is my Reward, with whom to live is my Joy, and to die is my Gain, tho' I had not had your forty-eight Hours Warning, for the Preparation of the Death of Mary Dyar.

And know this also, that if through the Enmity you shall declare yourselves worse than Ahasueras, and confirm your Law, tho' it were but the taking away the Life of one of us, That the Lord will overthrow both your Law and you, by his righteous Judgments and Plagues poured justly upon you, who now whilst you are warned thereof, and tenderly sought unto, may avoid the one, by removing the other; If you neither hear nor obey the Lord nor his Servants, yet will he send more of his Servants among you, so that your End shall be frustrated, that think to restrain them, you call "Cursed Quakers" from coming among you, by any Thing you can do to them; yea, verily, he hath a Seed here among you, for whom we have suffered all this while, and yet suffer: whom the Lord of the Harvest will send forth more Labourers to gather (out of the Mouths of the Devourers of all sorts) into his Fold, where he will lead them into fresh Pastures, even the Paths of Righteousness, for his Name's Sake: Oh! let none of you put this Day far from you, which verily in the light of the Lord I see approaching, even to many in and about Boston, which is the bitterest and darkest professing Place, and so to continue as long as you have done, that ever I heard of; let the time past therefore suffice, for such a Profession as bring forth such Fruits as these Laws are, In Love and in the Spirit of Meekness, I again beseech you, for I have no Enmity to the Persons of any; but you shall know, that God will not be mocked, but what you sow, that shall you reap from him, that will render to everyone according to the Deeds done in the Body, whether Good or Evil, Even so be it, saith

Mary Dyar[2]

News of the proposed hangings was traveling fast and protests were piling high. Thomas Temple, Governor of Acadia and Nova Scotia, wrote begging for the lives of the prisoners, and volunteering to take them to Nova Scotia at his own expense and give them homes and "land to plant on so they could provide for themselves."[3] He further volunteered to take the responsibility of fetching them if they ever attempted to return to Massachusetts.

Governor John Winthrop, Jr. of Connecticut, son of the late Governor of Massachusetts, came before the Massachusetts General Court to plead for the prisoners. Although he had banished Mary Dyer from Connecticut where she was preaching the year before, he said he would crawl on his bare knees from New Haven to Boston begging that the condemned would not be hanged and offering them shelter in Connecticut.

The most excited people were the inhabitants from around Boston. Although it had been an object of the rulers of Massachusetts to prevent the colonists from conversing with prisoners, the sympathy of the people grew stronger than the word of the rulers during the week before the hanging. They flocked to the prison windows to hear the victims speak, and the guards were unable to hold them back.

When William Dyer heard the news, he felt he had lost. He had received no answer from his letter to the Boston General Court. His son, Will, Jr., found him with head bowed in his folded arms. William explained to his son his stormy reservations about going to Boston again. Will, Jr. thought for a moment. He stood tall and straight, looking over-serious for his eighteen years, when he volunteered to go to the Boston magistrates and implore them to have compassion for his mother. William was concerned that his son might be arrested as a Quaker, but Will assured him that he was not known to be a Quaker, and he had never given his word of honor that his mother would keep out of Massachusetts.

William appealed to his son to do anything he could to bring her home where she belonged, confessing that he thought Mary was carried away at the moment, but she would change. Will Jr. shook hands with his father in confirmation of the plan. Will was captain of a frigate, already loaded with wares prepared to sail to the Azores. He hastened to board his ship and detour to Boston to rescue his mother before sailing overseas.

The day before the scheduled hanging, Governor Endicott had an unexpected caller. The handsome young man at his door announced that he was Will Dyer, Jr., the son of William and Mary. He had come instead of his father. Governor Endicott was impressed by the earnestness of this young man. He invited him to talk and called Rev. John Norton to join them. For some time they discussed Mary Dyer, agreeing that if she got close enough to the gallows it would give her the scare she needed to reform and stay away from Boston. Norton summed it up, "We will frighten her by bringing her to death's door. She needs to experience the chill of death to get some sense in her head."

Considering this possibility, they decided on a secret plan for the morrow. In the meantime, Will volunteered to visit his mother in the House of Correction that night and try to persuade her not to go through with the foolhardy act.

Mary Dyer was startled when her son walked into her cell. Nothing could have served better to illustrate the conflict of her life. Here was her own son pleading for the life she had already promised the Lord. She was torn between her Father in Heaven and her son on earth. Her heart started to rip; but she knew she must stop the tear. She would try to make Will understand. In a way, it was a comfort to have her son with her, but she wished he would leave. The Lord was trying her, and she must gather all of her strength to meet the challenge. Will stayed until the early morning. As he put his arms around Mary for a delayed embrace, it felt for a moment as if they were just another mother and son in a bizarre world. The minute they broke their embrace, Will sped from the House of Correction back to his ship in the harbor.

Mary wished that she had not been kept apart from Marmaduke Stevenson, William Robinson, and the other Quakers who were in the Boston jail. She yearned for one last talk with Christopher Holder before he sailed for England. His fiancée, Mary Scott, was among the nine other Quakers in jail. Mary could hear a racket from their direction. She knew something must be going on.

William Robinson had managed to put his head out the window of his upper room in the jail and speak to the people who had flocked on the street below. Captain James Oliver had tried to break up the group, galloping in with a company of men, but there were so many people gathered to hear what William Robinson had to say that it was impossible to disperse the crowd. Captain Oliver realized that he would have to resort to other means. Entering the prison in a fury, he hurled and pushed the imprisoned Friends downstairs to a "little low, dark cell, where [they] could not see the people." Besides Christopher Holder and Mary Scott, they were Robert Harper, William King, Mary Tresk, Provided Southwick, Hannah Phelps, Hope Clifton, and Daniel Gould. They sat together in the dark cell. Daniel Gould kept a diary in which he wrote:

It was a time of love; for as the world hated us and despitefully used us, so the Lord was pleased in a wonderful manner, to manifest his supporting love and kindness to us in our innocent sufferings; especially to the worthies who had now neared their course — for God had given them a sure word, that their souls should rest in eternal peace...

The same afternoon of October 27, 1659, Marshal Michaelson stopped to pick up William Robinson and Marmaduke Stevenson at the jail, and Mary Dyer at the House of Correction. From there, it was a mile's walk to the gallows. On every corner, town criers stood announcing the news. People were streaming in from all the outlying towns, bringing their children as a treat to the scene. Captain James Oliver tried to avoid some of the excitement by leading the prisoners down a back way, escorted by a band of 200 armed men beating their drums to drown out anyone who attempted to speak to the prisoners.

Walking hand in hand between William Robinson and Marmaduke Stevenson, Mary Dyer proceeded to march to the gallows. Marshal Michaelson asked Mary Dyer, "Are you not ashamed to walk hand in hand with two young men?"

As Mary Dyer started to reply, Captain Oliver ordered his men to beat their drums louder to drown out her voice. She could still be heard by some to say, "No, this is to me an hour of the greatest joy I could enjoy in the world. No eye can see, no ear can hear, no tongue can utter, and no heart can understand the sweet incomings, and refreshings of the Spirit of the Lord which now I feel."

"Drums beat louder," ordered the anxious Captain Oliver.

The three prisoners walked on with great cheerfulness. The two men were still wearing their hats. As they approached the gallows, Mary gave one startled look at John Wilson, the man who had received her into the Boston Church and baptized her son, Samuel, twenty-four years ago. Wilson leaned down from the horse he was riding and asked Robinson in a taunting manner, "Shall such jacks as you come in before authority with your hats on?"

Robinson had a quick reply. "Mind you, mind you, is it not for the putting on of hats that we are put to death?" As they came to the ladder, they took leave of each other with tender embraces. Robinson was the first to go cheerfully up the ladder, addressing the people.

"This is the day of your visitation, wherein the Lord hath visited you. This is the day the Lord is risen in his mighty power, to be avenged on all his adversaries. I suffer not as an evil doer. Mind the light that is within you; to with the Light of Christ, of which He testified and I am now going to seal with my blood".

Wilson became so incensed at what Robinson was saying that he said, "Hold thy tongue, be silent thou art going to die with a lie in thy mouth." The executioner bound Robinson's legs and arms, placed a neckcloth over his face and arranged the rope around his neck. Robinson had more to say, "Now ye are made manifest; I suffer for Christ in whom I live and in whom I die." There was a jerk of the rope, and Robinson was dead.

Marmaduke Stevenson was the next to step up on the ladder. He said, "Be it known to all this day, that we suffer not as evil doers, but for conscience sake; this day shall be at rest with the Lord." And so saying, the ladder was pulled out from under him.

Mary Dyer, seeing her companions hanging dead before her, stepped up on the ladder. Her skirts were tied around her feet. The halter was slipped over her head and lay limp on her neck. Her face was then covered with a handkerchief which the minister, John Wilson, had lent the hangman. As she stood on the ladder awaiting that final moment of death, there was suddenly a stir in the paralyzed crowd. A white horse came galloping across Boston Commons headed for the gallows. Its rider was wildly waving his hands and crying, "Stop! She is reprieved!"

A hundred voices shouted, "A reprieve!" Mary's feet were loosened, and the rope removed from her neck. When Wilson's handkerchief was removed she was startled to see her son Will holding the reprieve from Governor Endicott. Captain Oliver told her to come down off the ladder. Mary stood still and announced that she was still willing to suffer as her brethren, unless the wicked laws were annulled. Captain Oliver reminded her that it was for her son's sake that she was being spared. Mary was in such a stupendous state of shock that it became necessary for Marshall Michaelson to pick her up in his arms and carry her back to the prison. Will was standing in front of the jail, ready to give his mother one big embrace before leaving to board his vessel loaded with hogs and horses. He would like to have escorted his mother home, but he was needed on board as captain and, having accomplished his mission, he was filled with a sense of relief tempered with dread. Before boarding his frigate, Will reached in his pocket for the paper he would show his father on his return to Newport. It read:

> Whereas Mary Dyer is condemned by the General Court to be executed for her offenses, on the petition of William Dyer, her son, it is ordered that the said Mary Dyer shall have liberty for 48 hours after this day to depart out of this jurisdiction after which time, being found herein she is forthwith executed, and in the meantime she is to be kept a close prisoner till her son, or some other be ready to carry her away within the aforesaid time. It is further ordered that she will be carried to the place of execution and there to stand upon the gallows with a rope about her neck, till the rest be executed, and then to return to the prison and remain as aforesaid.

After Will left her, Mary Dyer returned to her cell and wrote a second letter to the Massachusetts General Court.

> Once more to the General Court, Assembled in Boston, speaks Mary Dyar, even as before: My life is not accepted, neither availeth me, in Comparison of the Lives and Liberty of the Truth and Servants of the Living God, for which in the Bowels of Love and Meekness I sought you; yet nevertheless, with wicked Hands have you put two of them to Death, which makes me to feel, that the Mercies of the Wicked is Cruelty. I rather chuse to die than to live, as from you, as Guilty of their innocent Blood. Therefore, seeing my Request is hindered, I leave you to the Righteous Judge and Searcher of all Hearts, who, with the pure measure of Light he hath given to every Man to profit withal, will in his due time let you see whose Servants you are, and of whom you have taken Counsel, which desire you to search into: But all his counsel hath been slighted, and, you would none of his reproofs. Read your

Portion, Prov. 1:24 to 32. "For verily the Night cometh on you apace, wherein no Man can Work, in which you shall assuredly fall to your own Master, in Obedience to the Lord, whom I serve with my Spirit, and pity to your Souls, which you neither know nor pity: I can do no less than once more to warn you, to put away the Evil of your Doings, and Kiss the Son, the Light in you before his wrath be kindled in you; for where it is, nothing without you can help or deliver you out of his hand at all; and if these things be not so, then say, There hath been no prophet from the Lord sent amongst you: yet it is his Pleasure, by Things that are not, to bring to naught Things that are."

When I heard your last Order read, it was a disturbance unto me, that was so freely Offering up my life to him that give it me, and sent me hither to do, which Obedience being his own Work, he gloriously accompanied with his Presence, and Peace, and Love in me, in which I rested from my labour, till by your Order, and the People, I was so far disturbed, that I could not retain anymore of the words thereof, than that I should return to Prison, and there remain Forty and Eight hours; to which I submitted, finding nothing from the Lord to the contrary, that I may know what his Pleasure and Counsel is concerning me, on whom I wait therefore, for he is my Life, and the length of my Days, and as I said before, I came at his command, and go at His command.

Mary Dyar[4]

The magistrates did not pay much attention to this letter. John Wilson had written a bawdy ballad describing the hanging of William Robinson and Marmaduke Stevenson, and young boys were singing it in the streets. Emotions were at a pitch on all sides. It was feared that a rebellion would break loose unless Mary Dyer was made to leave Boston within 48 hours.

The excited crowd, returning from the hanging to the north end of Boston, was so great that the bridge leading them across the river collapsed tossing all the pedestrians into the water.

Mary Dyer was put in the charge of four horsemen. They followed her fifteen miles south of Boston. Then she was left in the custody of one man to escort her back to Rhode Island. She hastened to dismiss him, saying that she could find her own way home. She was glad to ride alone. With one trip canceled, she needed the solitude to start rescheduling her life between heaven and earth.

{ 23 }
Shelter Island[1]

Mary Dyer was out of danger, but neither she nor her family could be content. How could they welcome home a beloved who was reluctant to be reprieved from the gallows? And how could Mary make her family accept the imperatives of her spiritual calling? She could not forget the dangling bodies of William Robinson and Marmaduke Stevenson.

Mary longed for the opportunity to communicate with other Quakers. Her son, Will, was the only other Quaker convert in the family, and he was on his frigate headed towards the Azores.[2] It was much easier for Anne Hutchinson's sister, Catherine Scott, for she, her husband, Richard, and daughters, Mary and Patience, were united in their belief, and their home in Providence had become a center for Quaker meetings. Like Margaret Fell, Catherine Scott could combine faith and family without conflict.

The nearest Quakers to the Dyer Farm were Anne and William Coddington. Mary began to seek out their company more and more. It took Quakers to understand Quakers. This did not please William Dyer at all. He had suffered the Quakers distracting Mary from her family and he could not forget the past deviousness of Coddington in seizing the local power for himself. William must have felt a sense of helplessness when the Coddingtons invited his wife to sail with them to visit the Sylvesters on Shelter Island. Mary was unpredictable and William was right in being concerned over her activities, but he did not know just how right.

It was a nice day's sail across Long Island Sound. Shelter Island lay snug between the north and south forks of Long Island, its location descriptive of its name. But for Mary Dyer, it signified a spiritual shelter where her good friends, Christopher Holder, John

Rous, William Robinson, and Marmaduke Stevenson had all sought temporary refuge from the Puritan storms.

The Sylvesters had built their home overlooking a cove where boats could easily be moored stern-first to the banks. Nathaniel Sylvester was always on the lookout for approaching ships, and when he spotted the flapping white sails of the familiar pinnace tacking towards the inlet, he and Gissell came hurrying down to the water's edge. Anne Coddington was the first to leap on shore and embrace her younger sister. Living as they did on two such different islands, the Brinley sisters had a lot of daily details to exchange, but most important was the news from Holland concerning their father, Thomas Brinley, who had escorted Prince Charles on his escape from England at the time of the execution of Charles I.

Mary followed the two chattering sisters through hawthorne hedges, sweet-smelling boxwood, and luxurious rose gardens to "Woodstock," the home of the Sylvesters for the past seven years, six of which Mary had spent in England. She wondered how this young couple happened to settle on such an isolated island, independent of the other colony inhabitants.

In 1651 Nathaniel Sylvester had joined with three other sugar merchants from Barbados to purchase Shelter Island from the colony of New Haven for 1,600 pounds of "good" muscavado sugar. Of the four purchasers, Nathaniel was the only one interested in making it his home, and eventually he had became the sole owner. In 1652, he and his sixteen year-old English bride became the first white settlers on an island occupied only by Manhanset Indians. When Poggatucut, Sachem of the Manhansets, deeded his tribal domain to Nathanial Sylvester, he had no concept of what was going to happen to the land. In order to cultivate the land, Nathaniel imported slaves from Barbados to work side by side with the Native Americans. Both Indians and Negroes were housed together in cramped quarters. In contrast to the slave labor, the Indians were indentured and paid for their work, remaining free to leave the island. They continued to stay in touch with the Indians on Long Island, communicating by smoke signals. Many moved back to Long Island, finding the work in the large tobacco fields too arduous. The Africans proved to be in much better condition than the Indians for hard labor in the tobacco fields.

Having met George Fox just before they left England, the Sylvesters were very sympathetic and hospitable to all Quakers. But the Quaker ideals were opposed to slavery, and the number of slaves owned by both Gissell and Nathaniel must have created conflict.

Every Sunday, four slaves paddled the Sylvesters for six miles on a raft to attend church in Southold, Long Island. It was the only church in the Long Island area, founded in 1640 by John Youngs, a Puritan congregationalist minister who had first landed in Salem and moved to New Haven. The Southold settlement was started under the auspices of New Haven, carrying rigid provisions for persecution of heresy. Quakers were subject to whipping. We do not know whether Mary ever attended the Southold Church as guests of the Sylvesters. She probably would not have gone more than once, for Mary's sense of protest and challenge was now reserved for the central core of Puritan oligarchy. She was biding her time for the final thrust.

Mary was continually reminded of the message George Fox had sent to the colonies with Christopher Holder concerning "Black and Indian Slaves," warning that "every captured creature under the whole Heaven deserves liberty and freedom." How could God's universal message reach these toilers of the land, and how could they be helped to discover their own individual worth? These questions tormented Mary.

One day, just as the Coddingtons were preparing to return to Newport, a group of Indians approached Mary and asked if she would hold Quaker meetings with them. It was like an answer to a prayer. The Indians were then joined by the slaves in meeting with Mary in the forest.

What a sight they must have been amidst the massive spread of gigantic white oaks, the sun finding only the smallest peek holes to shine through and lighten the floor of the forest with shifting patterns, sensitive to each passing breeze. The English Quaker, the Native Americans, and the African slaves sat in a circle, overcome by their shared spirituality and unabashed by the dramatic dissimilarities of their backgrounds. Only the hands and face of Mary revealed the lightness of her skin. In contrast, the Indians displayed all of their bronzed, painted bodies, decked with beads and feathers. Enhancing those bright colors, the rich blackness of the African skin shone to reveal the hardened bulges of their disciplined muscles.

It was a time of profound satisfaction for Mary. By seeking her out, the Indians had set up an experience for Mary which was quite different from that of the two Englishmen who had dedicated their lives to becoming prophets to the Indians. In Massachusetts, John Eliot tried to remould the Algonquin Indians into Englishmen, while in Rhode Island, Roger Williams devoted his efforts to helping Englishmen understand the Narragansett Indians.[3] It was one of Roger's greatest disappointments that the Indians never adopted one God, but, out of love for Roger, merely added "his God' to their assortment of some thirty-eight other deities.[4] Mary had no need or desire to be dictatorial, like John Eliot, or condescending, like Roger Williams. Her meetings with the Indians were spontaneous and free from the need of reinforcements.

It was a very private experience, but Mary had one visitor who has left a journal describing a meeting he attended. John Taylor was a sugar trader from Barbados who had become a Quaker in 1656 when he met George Fox in England. On one of his expeditions to Long Island Sound, he had occasion to attend Mary's meetings with the Indians on Shelter Island. John Taylor wrote of "a comely woman and a grave matron who even shined in the image of God, we had several brave meetings there [in Shelter Island] together, and the Lord's power and preference were with us generously."[5]

Mary might have remained for many months in her shining role on this remote island where God's message faced no disturbance, but the powers still remained in Boston to destroy such a haven. She was bitterly reminded when Nathaniel and Patience Southwick arrived on Shelter Island. The Southwicks were Quakers who had been badly beaten along with their teenage children in the Salem jail. As they had not been able to pay for the "rent" of their confinement, the Boston magistrates ordered the Southwick children to be sent as slaves to Barbados. Although sea captains were accustomed to transporting slaves from Barbados to New England, and Indians as slaves from the Colonies, no barque or pinnace would take the

Southwick children to become slaves. Banished from Massachusetts, Nathaniel and Patience became so depressed and exhausted with fear over the outcome of their children that they soon died. Mary was with them when they died. Her sense of protest was overwhelming. The hearts hanged on Shelter Island were analogous to the deaths she had witnessed on Boston Commons. Nothing had improved in Massachusetts; cruelty was on the increase and the opportunity for the word of God to be heard was on the decline. What was she doing lingering in this beautiful speck of an island fulfilled by such a tiny sample of humanity.

Every day, Mary walked the shores of Shelter Island in deep contemplation. Just as the waves advanced on the silence of the sands, the voice of God invaded the quiet of her soul's shore. She kept repeating to herself the words of George Fox, "continuity of silence restores the ability to hear." The peace on Shelter Island was like the eye of the storm. Mary gained fresh realization that God had intended her to confront the hurricane.

As Mary was contemplating her decision, word came from Boston that Governor Endicott, the magistrates and ministers, were boasting of her reprieve to justify their existence. A Declaration of the General Court of Massachusetts was to be sent to England for circulation, explaining and justifying the attitude of the Boston magistrates towards the Quakers. England was so far away. How could she ever expect them to learn what really happened? Governor Endicott was squirming out of his responsibilities. Mary read the following document with a sense of fury:

Although the justice of our proceedings against William Robinson, Marmaduke Stevenson, and Mary Dyer, supported by the authority of this Court, the lawes of the country; and the law of God, may rather persuade us to expect incouragement and commendation from all prudent and pious men, then convince us of any necessity to Apologize for the same, yet for as much as men of weaker parts, out of pity and comiseration (a commendable Christian virtue yet easily abused, and susceptible of sinister and dangerous impressions) for want of full information, may be left satisfied, and men of perverser principles, may take occasion hereby to columniate us, and render us as bloody persecutors, to satisfy the one, and stop the mouths of the other, we thought it requisite to declare,

That about three years since, divers persons, professing themselves Quakers (of whose pernicious Opinions and Practices we have received intelligence from good hands from Barbados to England) arrived at Boston whose persons were only secured, to be sent away by the first opportunity, without censure or punishment, although their professed tenents, turbulent and contemptuous behavior to Authority would have justified a severer animadversion, yet the prudence of this Court, was exercised only in making provision to secure the Peace and order here established, against their attempts, whose design (we were well assured of by our own experience, as well as by the example of their predecessors in Munster) was to undermine and ruine the same.

And accordingly a law was made and published, prohibiting all Masters of Ships, to bring any Quaker into his jurisdiction, and themselves from coming in, on penalty of the House of Correction, till they could be sent away; notwithstanding which, by a back Door, they found entrance, and the penalty inflicted on themselves, proving insufficient to restrain their impudent and insolent obtrusions, was increased by the loss of the ears of those that offended the second time, which also being too weak a defence against their impetuous frantick fury, necessitated us to endeavor our security, and upon serious consideration, after the former experiments, by their incessant assaults, a Law was made, that such persons should be banished, on pain of Death, according to the example of England in their provision against Jesuits, which sentence being regularly pronounced at the last Court of Assistant against the parties above named, and they either returning, or continuing presumptuously in this Jurisdiction, after the time limited, were apprehended, and owning themselves to be persons banished, were sentenced (by the Court) to death, according to the law aforesaid, which hath been executed upon two of them;

Mary Dyer upon the petition of her Son, and the mercy and clemency of this Court, had liberty to depart within two days, which she had accepted of the consideration of our gradual proceeding, will vindicate us from the clamorous accusations of severity, our own just and necessary defence, calling upon us (other means fayling) to offer the poynt, which these persons have violently, and wilfully rushed upon, and thereby become "felons de se," which might it have been prevented, and the sovereign law 's alue populi' been preserved, our former proceedings, as well as the sparing of Mary Dyer, upon an inconsiderable intercession, will manifestly evince.

We desire their lives absent, rather than their death present.

November 18, 1659   Edward Rawson, secretary[6]

Mary contemplated the lies of this document which would be circulated in England. There had been no change in the bloody laws and Mary's reprieve was serving as a deceit to the whole world. Lies sailed faster than truth across the Atlantic. The Boston authorities must not be allowed to stand behind this fraud. Mary could not address Governor Endicott from Shelter Island; she must return to Boston. She could not leave her life as a lie. As she was to say in defense of her final decision, "My life not availeth me in comparison to the liberty of the truth."[7]

It was late in April 1660, when Mary Dyer left Shelter Island to challenge Boston once more. She did not dare risk sharing the purpose of her departure with the Sylvesters. They were too close to the Coddingtons. She procured a horse to ferry to Long Island and she made her way through unfamiliar Indian territory to the western tip of Long Island, where she could ferry to Rhode Island. Changing horses in Narragansett, she proceeded to Providence where she could rest for a few days with the Scotts, knowing she could depend on their secrecy. It was comforting for Mary to be with Anne Hutchinson's sister; but for Catherine Scott, it was heart rending to watch her friend so bravely leaving Rhode Island forever, headed straight for the lion's den.

{ 24 }
Hangs Like A Flag

It took a week for the news to reach William Dyer that Mary Dyer had left Shelter Island, slipped by Providence, and had arrived in Boston once again. This desertion was beginning to look more permanent — frighteningly so. Mary's guiding inner light was quite beyond the reach of William. He was deeply in favor of freedom of conscience, and it would have been against his principles to object; but how had the Quakers ever gotten such a hold on his wife? It made him feel very lonely to witness her enlightenment by some force so completely removed from his sphere of influence. He had hoped that this was a temporary phase, but she was taking the separation too far. Yet, in spite of all the differences which had developed over the twenty-seven years of marriage, that initial bond of love was indestructible. William would have given anything, done anything, just to have Mary back. In his deep despair, he searched his soul for prompting. Now that Mary was in Boston, she was really at the mercy of Governor Endicott. His letter of nine months ago had influenced the General Court sufficiently to prevent her death. The General Court had not changed its bloody laws, and William knew that that was his wife's mission. They were inexcusable laws, but no law was worthy of the sacrifice of the life of his wife. The only thing he could think of doing was to write to Governor Endicott again. This was to be a different kind of letter from the earlier one. He would not irritate their sense of guilt as Puritans. He would not mock their inhumanity as caretakers. He would not even challenge their lawlessness as statesmen. This time, William Dyer would appeal to those Boston magistrates simply as lovers of women:

Honor S',
    It is no little greif of mind, and sadness of hart that I am

necessitated to be so bold as to supplicate yo' Honor self w' the
Honorable Assembly of yo' Generall Courte to extend yo' mercy
and favo' once agen to me and my children, little did I dream that I
shuld have had occasion to petiton you in a matter of this nature,
but so it is that throw the devine prouidence and yo' benignity my
sonn obtayned so much pitty and mercy att yo' hands as to enjoy
the life of his mother, now my supplicaton yo' Hono' is to begg
affectionately, the life of my deare wife, tis true I have not seen
her aboue this half yeare and therefor cannot tell how in the frame
of her spiritt she was moved thus againe to runn so great a Hazard
to herself, and perplexity to me and mine and all her friends and
well wishers; so itt is from Shelter Island about by Pequid
Narragansett and to the Towne of Prouidence she secrettly and
speedyly journyed, and as secretly from thence came to yo'
jurisdiction, unhappy journy may I say, and woe to theat generat-
con say I that gives occasion thus of grief and troble (to those that
desire to be quiett) by helping one another (as I may say) to
Hazard their lives for I know not watt end or to what purpose; If
her zeale be so greatt as thus to adventure, oh lett your favoure
and pitty surmount itt and save her life. Let not yo' forwanted
Compassion bee conquared by her inconsiderate maddnesse, and
how greatly will yo' renowne be spread if by so conquering yo'
become victorious, what shall I say more, I know yo' are all
sensible of my condition, and lett the reflect bee, and you will see
whatt my peticon is and what will give me and mine peace, oh
Lett mercies wings once more sore above justice ballance, and
then whilst I live shall I exalt yo' goodness butt other wayes twill
be a languishing sorrow, yea so great that I shuld gladly suffer thie
blow att once much rather: I shall forebear to troble yo' Hn' with
words neythe am I in capacity to expatiate myself at present; I
only say that yo'selves have been and are or may bee husbands to
wife or wiues, so am I: yea to one most dearely beloved: oh do not
you deprive me of her, but I pray give her me once agen and I
shall bee so much obleiged for ever, that I shall endeavor
continually to utter my thanks and render you Love and Honor
most renowned: pitty me, I begg itt with teares, and rest you.

Most humbly suppliant
W. Dyre

Portsmouth 27 of [May] 1660

Most honored sirs, let these lines by yo' fauo' bee my Peticon to your Honorable General Court at present sitting.

W. D.

He gave the letter to a swift-footed Indian to deliver to Boston.

Governor Endicott received William Dyer's letter and presented it to the General Court. Too bad if William Dyer was having trouble with his wife. She was giving them trouble too. She had no right to come back and defy their orders. She had been given her just warning. This was too much. Mary Dyer had been in Boston ten days, and it was time to call her before the General Court for one last inquisition. She was summoned to appear on May 31, 1660.

Mary Dyer entered the General Court looking a little greyer, and a little older than the year before. She was now forty-nine. Her changed appearance confused Governor Endicott. He was not certain it was that same woman. He looked her over questioningly. "Are you the same Mary Dyer that was here before?"

Mary Dyer: "I am the same Mary Dyer that was here at the last General Court."

Governor Endicott: "You will own yourself a Quaker, will you not?"

Mary Dyer stiffened. "I am myself to be reproachfully called so."

The jailer exclaimed, "She is a vagabond!"

Governor Endicott continued, "The sentence was passed upon you by the General Court and now likewise; you must return to the prison and there remain until tomorrow at nine o'clock; then from thence you must go to the gallows, and there be hanged till you are dead."

Mary Dyer did not flinch. "This is no more than what you said before."

Governor Endicott: "But now it is to be executed; therefore prepare yourself tomorrow at nine o'clock."

Mary Dyer: "I came in obedience to the will of God to the last

General Court desiring you to appeal your unrighteous laws of
banishment on pain of death; and that same is my work now, and
earnest request, although I told you that if you refused to repeal them,
the Lord would send others of his servants to witness against them."

Governor Endicott puzzled, "Are you a prophetess?"

Mary Dyer: "I speak the words that the Lord speaks in me and
now the thing has come to pass." She began to speak of her callings,
but was shut off.

Governor Endicott was at his saturation point. He stood up in
anger and, waving to the prison guard, he yelled, "Away with her!
Away with her!"

The guard took Mary Dyer by the arm and escorted her back to
prison. She was watched carefully despite her protests and requests to
be left alone. The window was blocked so that she could not
communicate with all the people standing in curiosity and consideration outside her cell, but as the night drew on, all of her sensibilities
must have been consumed by her flame within.

At the appointed time of nine o'clock the next morning, June the
first, Marshall Michaelson entered her room to fetch her out. Mary
Dyer asked him to wait outside for just a little. She said that she
would be ready presently. Marshal Michaelson was granting no
courtesies. He thundered, "Wait for you? I cannot wait for you! You
should wait upon me!"

At this point, Mary Dyer was hurried out of the prison where a
band of soldiers was ready to escort her to the gallows. It was a one-
mile walk through Boston from the jail to the Commons. The
Magistrates were very apprehensive that the gathering crowd might
become uncontrollably compassionate and they took every precau-
tion to cut off communication between Mary Dyer and her followers.
Led through the streets sandwiched between drummers, with
constant rat-a-tat-tat in front, followed by a persistent rat-a-tat-tat
behind, Mary Dyer walked to her death. Some of the followers were
able to defy the drummers and militant marchers by moving close to
Mary Dyer and pleading, "Mary Dyer, don't die. Go back to Rhode
Island where you might save your life. We beg of you, go back! Go
back and live!"

Raising her voice above the hammering of the drummers, she said, "Nay, I cannot go back to Rhode Island, for in obedience to the will of the Lord I came, and in His will I abide faithful to death."

As Mary Dyer reached the place of execution, close to Frog Pond by the great elm tree in Boston Commons, the drums were quieted and Captain John Webb spoke up. Turning to the agitated crowd in justification, he said, "She has been here before and had the sentence of banishment upon pain of death and has broken the law in coming again now. It is therefore she who is guilty of her own blood."

Mary Dyer spoke in contradiction, "Nay, I came to keep bloodguiltiness from you, desiring you to repeal the unrighteous and unjust laws of banishment upon pain of death made against the innocent servants of the Lord. Therefore, my blood will be required at your hands who wilfully do it." She was addressing Captain John Webb, Mr. Simon Bradstreet, Pastor John Wilson, and his assistant, Mr. John North, who were all clustered together. She then spread out her arms towards the outlying crowd and said, "But, for those who do it in the simplicity of their hearts, I desire the Lord to forgive them. I came to do the will of my father, and in obedience to this will I stand even to death." Pastor Wilson started to shudder. He clenched his fists and cried, "Mary Dyer, O repent, O repent, and be not so deluded and carried away by the deceit of the devil." Mary Dyer looked directly at Mr. Wilson and said decisively, "Nay, man, I am not now to repent."

John Norton stepped forward and asked, "Would you have the elders pray for you?" Mary Dyer responded, "I desire the prayer of all the people of God." A voice from the crowd called out, "It may be that she thinks there is none here." John Norton pleaded, "Are you sure you don't want one of the elders to pray for you?" Mary Dyer answered, "Nay, first a child, then a young man, then a strong man, before an elder in Christ Jesus."

Someone from the crowd called out, "Did you say you have been in Paradise?" Mary Dyer acclaimed, "Yea, I have been in Paradise several days and now I am about to enter eternal happiness." Captain John Webb signalled to Edward Wanton, officer of the gallows, who adjusted the noose hanging from the great elm tree and moved the ladder under it. Mary Dyer needed no assistance in mounting the scaffold. With a smile lighting up her face, step by step, she ascended the rickety wooden structure.

Mr. Wilson had his large handkerchief ready to place over her head. No one would have to see that look of rapture twisted to distortion — only the dangling body. As her neck snapped, the crowd stood paralyzed in the silence of death until a spring breeze lifted her limp skirt until it billowed in response. General Atherton cracked the silence, "She hangs like a flag," he said. A chorus of voices repeated, "Ay, she hangs like a flag." And one strong voice continued, "She hangs like a flag for others to take example from."

Edward Wanton vomited in Frog Pond three times before he could mount his steed. As he trotted past the great elm tree, his horse whinnied, reared, and almost threw him to the ground. He pressed his heels and hurried home. Once inside his mother's house, he threw down his musket and halberd. Sinking his head in his arms he sobbed, "Alas Mother! We have been murdering the Lord's people," and taking off his sword, he made a vow never to wear it again. Not long after, he became a member of the Society of Friends and two years later he was arrested for holding Quaker meetings in his house.

* * *

Despite all the frantic attempts of the Boston magistrates to rid themselves of the challenging Quakers, they failed. Although they could hang Mary Dyer, they could not rid Boston of her presence. Three hundred years later, she returned to sit in bronze in front of the Boston State House, with the statement she made in the Boston jail engraved for everyone to read as they walk down Beacon Street:

> My Life not Availeth Me
> In Comparison to
> The Liberty of the Truth

21. The bronze of Mary Dyer by Sylvia Shaw Judson in front of the Boston State House (photo by Dara Pannebaker).

{ 25 }
Aftermath of Mary's Hanging

T he hanging of Mary Dyer was instant news for Boston, spreading as fast as an Indian could run to Rhode Island and as slowly as the next brig could sail to England.

A gripping account of the impact on Anne Bradstreet has been left for us by John Greenleaf Whittier, who describes Anne on the day of the hearing as "so wrought up that she was fain to take to her bed, refusing to be comforted, and counting it the heaviest day of her life."[1] When she heard the crowd returning from the hanging on Boston Commons, she cried out, "The hoof-print of every horse falls right upon my heart!" Presently Simon Bradstreet returned home, the man she had formerly addressed so joyfully, "If ever two were one, then surely we. If ever man were loved by wife, than thee."[2] Now she saw him as the magistrate most responsible for the decision to hang Mary Dyer. Anne's whisper was choked with grief. "Simon," she wept, "But might not life be spared" Death is a great thing!"

In the past, Anne Bradstreet had turned to poetry to clear her emotions, describing in detail such as the total burning of her house in Andover, but she could not write about the hanging of Mary Dyer. This day her quill was stilled.

What was the response of the seven remaining members of Mary's family to her hanging? There is no record of their expressions of grief and anger.[3] However, Mary's next-door neighbor in Newport, Anne Brinley Coddington, has left us a letter expressing her feelings. Accustomed as she was to having her husband, William Coddington, correspond with heads of state, a month after the hanging of her friend, Mary Dyer, Anne Brinley Coddington wrote the following letter to Governor Endicott, the deputy governor and the rest of the magistrates:

Friends!

It is so with me that I cannot any longer forbear to give you Warning of the Evil of your Ways, that you are now walking in, both in making and putting in Execution that cruel and wicked Law of yours, in punishing and putting to Death those that for Confidence-sake among you do declare the Word of the Lord; but you, instead of hearkening unto them, both whip, cut the Ears, and have put to Death three of them, in your own Will, and not in the Will of the Lord: But put the Case, you say *They are Here-ticks, and such ought to die*. To that I answer, You will profess that you are *Christians*, and walk according to the Commands of Christ; if so, where will you find, that Christ commanded such to be put to Death? Did not he say, that the *Tares should grow among the Wheat until the Harvest?* And now who are you that judge another Man's Servant, who must stand or fall to his own Master' Neither do ye follow the Apostle's Rule, who said, *With sound Doctrine the Gainsayers must be convinced;* but you Magistrates of Boston not being armed with spiritual Weapons, as good Soldiers of *Christ Jesus*, take not up the Sword of the Spirit, which is the Word of God, but use his weapons from ye serve, which are Whips, Knives, and Halters; you are just of his Mind, nothing will serve your Turns, nor justify your Malice, but their Lives: You are ready to plead as your Master did against *Job, Skin for Skin, all that a Man hath will he give for his Life*: So that it was *Job's Life* that he would have had, had the Lord permitted, as he hath done to you, that ye may fill up the Measure of your Cruelty. Would you not have thought it hard Measure, if any of you had been used so by the Bishops' Nay, did you not so think, though they did less than you yourselves have done' Is this the following the Command of Christ, who said, *Whatsoever ye would that Men would do unto you, that do unto them?* But you will say, *They break your Laws:* Well, consider which of you hath not broke the Law of God: Have you not had other Gods besides him' Yea, the Gods whom ye serve, and whose Commands ye have obeyed. Are not your Priests your Gods whom ye have chosen' And their Commands ye have followed in this very Thing: I now appeal to your Consciences, if it be not so; for though they speak *Peace,* yet if a *Man put not into their Mouths, they prepare for War.* And are you not like them in *Micab iii.10?* Do you now *build up* your Church *with Blood,* and your Town *with Iniquity*'? for the Heads thereof *judge for Reward,* and the *Priests* thereof *teach for Hire,* and the *Prophets* thereof *divine for Money,* yet will they lean upon the Lord and say, *Is not the Lord among us*'?*None Evil can come upon us. Secondly,* Do you not make *Graven Images?* Yea, of yourselves, and of your Laws, that they who will not honor you, and keep your Laws, though it goes against their Conscience, you have like *Nebuchadnezzar* made *one Law,* that is *to put to Death.* So that now you see, that your Craft and your Dissembling about your making your Laws cannot any longer be hid. Now therefore, while it is yet Time and Place for Repentance, repent and judge righteously, for Judgment is not Man's but God's. Oh! let not the Cries of the Fatherles and Widow come against you, for their Redeemer is mighty, that will plead their Cause; and as you have thirsted after Blood, you shall have Blood given you to drink, unless you prepare to meet the Lord by timely Repentance, yea, that Repentance which is never to be repented of: For Blood is a crying Sin: It cries loud in the Ears of the Lord for Vengeance as the Blood of *Abel* cried to the Lord from the Earth. And will you remain in *Cain's* Nature, to persecute and slay the Servants of the Most High. that are sent to you' Oh! take Warning betimes, lest Repentance be had from your Eyes. Truly this Burden lay upon me from the Lord to declare unto you, and I, like *Jonah,* was not willing to have declared it, and the Lord hath afflicted me for it; but now being warned the second Time, I could no longer forbear, for it was in me like new Wine and hath *no Vent.* Oh, therefore be warned by one who is a Friend unto you, and Well-wisher of the Health and Prosperity of your Souls.

Rhode Island, July 7th 1660   ANNE CODDINGTON[4]

While Anne Coddington expressed her rage directly to Governor Endicott, her husband reached out in a different direction for consolation. Recalling the statement of John Winthrop, Jr., Governor of Connecticut, that he would have crawled on his bare knees from Hartford to Boston if he could have possibly prevented the hanging of Mary Dyer, William Coddington wrote four letters to Winthrop, his quill crawling like bare knees in pain and humility. Several years later, the Coddingtons opened their home to become the first Quaker Meeting House in Newport.

The impact of the news in England was even more profound than in the Colonies. Three days before the hanging of Mary Dyer, London had gone wild with celebration for the return of Charles II. After fourteen years of exile, he came home on his thirtieth birthday. Eleven years of parliamentary rule had been enough for the English. Everyone was embracing, dancing in the streets, and shouting, "Royalty restored! Long live the King!" Mary Dyer's mentor, George Fox, was confined to his cell at Lancaster Castle. On the day of Mary's hanging, he confided to his journal that he was receiving vibrations of a Quaker disaster in Boston.[5] Two weeks after the extravaganza on the streets of London, George Fox wrote a letter of warning to King Charles II.

Oh it is hard to utter how much wine and strong drink hath been devoured in waste by people drinking of healths to thee, some upon their knees, and some otherwise, even until some hath been so drunk, they could neither speak or go right, and what abundance of wood have been wasted and devoured of great bon fires (as they call them) which they have done as they say to rejoice because of thee coming, yes even such great fires had been dangerous to the cities and townes, and such noises have been heard and scarce even have been the like, by shooting off of guns great and small and by ringing of bells and by people singing and laughing and shouting like histerical mad men in the streets and several places strewn with flowers and the like; and this is done in rejoicing concerning thee, and what abundance hath been devoured in feasting, and banqueting and abominable rejoicing?

And also consider in what great need poor people are in ... consider what can be the end of all these things ... I have beheld the danger which thou are in which is exceedingly great.

The news of Mary's hanging gradually reached other countries. It was reported in the Swarthmore manuscripts that Mary Dyer "cast back the suggestions of mercy in the face of the judge and demanded only justice."[6]

Then again in Ireland, Mary was referred to as "a lively testimony of the virtues of the truth, which can look death in the face, and be a record for future generations."[7]

And when news of the hanging reached Paris, the French had their own way of responding: "Ainsi; Mary Dyer donna sa vie pour le salient de ses frères; ce qui doit lui assurer une place parmi la grande femme d'Amerique, n'est-elle pas fait autre chose."[8]

John Taylor, who had recently been with Mary, wrote in his journal: "And Mary went away [from Shelter Island] for Boston again and said she must go and offer her life there, and desire them to repeal the wicked law which they had made against God's people, — she sealed her testimony with her blood; and so conquered through Death, and is gone into eternal life."

The news and manner of Mary's death needed to be brought to the attention of the King. Samuel Shattuck, who had remained an ardent Quaker ever since he removed the glove from Christopher Holder's throat in the Salem Church, took on the commission. In 1661, he was banished "on pain of death" from the Massachusetts Bay Colony. Just before he sailed for England, William Leddra was hanged. Leddra was the fourth Quaker to be sent to the gallows on Boston Commons. When Samuel Shattuck landed in London, he got in touch with his good friend Christopher Holder, and they gathered together with Edward Burroughs and George Fox, who had recently been released from jail, to discuss what could be done about the Boston hangings.[9]

Edward Burroughs was selected to approach King Charles II. He hurried for an appointment, pressing the urgency of his request, "for we know not how many [more] may soon be put to death."

The name of Mary Dyer was not unknown to King Charles II. His accountant, Thomas Brinley, had heard the news from his daughters. Anne Brinley Coddington wrote to report to her father at the same time she wrote to protest Governor Endicott. Gissell Brinley Sylvester had written her father about Mary's visit to Shelter Island directly before her hanging.

King Charles II was quick to respond to Burrough's request that such hangings should not be allowed in Boston. The letter he wrote Governor Endicott indicated that England was in a far better situation to deal with the Quakers than Massachusetts Bay Colony.

Given at our court at Whitehall the 9th day of September 1661.

By his majesty's command, William Morris.

Sent to our truly and well beloved John Endicott, esq. and to all and every other Governor, or governments of our plantations of New England, and all the colonies thereunto belong: that now are here after shall be; and to all and every ministers and offices of our said Plantations in Colonies whosoever with the continent of New England.

Trusty and beloved, we greet you well. Having been informed that several of our subjects amongst you, called Quakers, have been and are imprisoned by you, whereof some have been executed, and others [as have been represented unto us] are in danger to undergo the like: we have thought fit to signify our pleasure in that behalf for the future; and do hereby require that if there be any of these people called Quakers amongst you, now already condemned to suffer death, or other corporal punishment, or that you are imprisoned, and obnoxious to the like condemnation, you are to forebear to proceed any further herein; but that you forewith send the said persons (whether condemned or imprisoned) over unto our Kingdom of England, together with the respective crime or offence laid to their charge; to the end that such course may be taken with them here, as shall be agreeable to our laws, and their demerits. And for so doing, these our letters shall be your sufficient warrant and discharge.

Edward Burroughs took the mandamus with eagerness and

thanked the King for his cooperation. He hurried to the port to find the quickest messenger to Boston, only to discover that no vessel was likely to sail there for some time. George Fox, Christopher Holder, and other concerned Friends offered to raise enough money to be donated to Ralph Goldsmith if he would sail his ship within ten days, with or without freight, to Boston. Ralph Goldsmith accepted the offer. They still needed a messenger to deliver the mandamus to Governor Endicott, and Edward Burroughs suggested that Samuel Shattuck, who had so recently been banned from Boston, would be a most appropriate messenger. Edward Burroughs went back to the King to ask if he would be willing to dispatch one called "a Quaker" to carry the mandamus to New England. The King thought this was an excellent scheme and Samuel Shattuck set sail accompanied by other Quakers late in September 1661 with the message from the King. Sailing with a "prosperous gale", they arrived in Boston in six weeks.

22. Whipping Quakers through the streets of Boston
(drawing by Sheppard--courtesy of The Bettmann Archive).

{ 26 }
Boston 1661

On a Sunday morning in November 1661, a year and a half after Mary's hanging, Ralph Goldsmith's vessel was spotted off the New England coast. The citizens of Boston were excited to see the ship sail into the harbor from England, and by the time Samuel Shattuck had lowered the anchor, several small boats were clustering around, anxious for news. Ralph Goldsmith and Samuel Shattuck had agreed on their crossing that no information should be given out or any letters delivered until they had gone ashore and delivered the mandamus to Governor Endicott. They would not embark on a Sunday, much to the disappointment of all the visitors in small boats. One man thought he recognized Samuel Shattuck sitting placidly on the stern of the ship, just as if he belonged in Boston Harbor. This report caused quite a stir in the town.

On Monday morning, Samuel Shattuck and Ralph Goldsmith were rowed ashore by other members of the Quaker crew, who were instructed to return and wait on the ship while they performed their royal errand.[1] Anxiety rustled through the streets as the two men walked assertively to Governor Endicott's house. Samuel Shattuck pulled his hat firmly over his forehead before knocking on the door. When Governor Endicott heard the knock he sent a servant to inquire. Upon hearing that the business was from the King of England and could be delivered to none other than the Governor himself, he permitted their entrance. Governor Endicott gave one look at Samuel Shattuck and ordered him to remove his hat. Samuel Shattuck did not stir. The servant then grabbed the hats off the heads of both visiting men and threw them on the floor. Governor Endicott could not tolerate disrespect and was quick to order the arrest of these two cocky men. Samuel Shattuck suggested gently that Governor Endicott might first read the King's message before arresting them. Withdrawing the precious document from his inner coat pocket, Samuel Shattuck handed it to the Governor. Endicott ripped open the contents, and when he saw the royal signature, he turned white. He read the royal mandamus and removed his own hat "in respect to being in the presence of a messenger of the King." Sheepishly, he asked his servant to return the hats on the floor to Samuel Shattuck and Ralph Goldsmith. The two Quakers tried to suppress their grins as they put on their hats. Governor Endicott reread the mandamus with studied concern and bade Samuel Shattuck and Ralph Goldsmith follow him while he consulted with his deputy governor, Richard Bellingham. The three men walked uncomfortably to Bellingham's house and Shattuck and Goldsmith waited outside while Endicott entered to confer privately with Bellingham. When Endicott returned to the waiting messengers, he solemnly announced, "We shall obey his majesty's command."

Samuel Shattuck and Ralph Goldsmith were light-footed as they returned to their ship and gave the other passengers permission to come ashore. The other Quakers landed and met with the Boston Friends to offer praise to God for their deliverance. There would be no more hangings on the Boston Commons. This was announced just in time to cancel the planned hanging of Winlock Christison the following day.

Governor Endicott's Council met and issued an order to the keeper of the prison to set at liberty all the Quakers in confinement. The Council then met in great consternation over the unexpected royal blow to their prestige. They feared that action might be taken against the colony for having gone beyond the authority granted in their charter, and they were apprehensive over the excitement which had been aroused in England over the Boston hangings. The Council resolved to send their minister, John Norton, and magistrate, Simon Bradstreet, to England to give an explanation for their activities, and to try and remove any unfavorable opinion.

John Norton and Simon Bradstreet set sail with a certain amount of fanfare as the Royal Commission to his Royal Highness, primed to reinstate the reputation of Massachusetts in England. They had not been back to England for many years and anticipated a warm and exciting reception.

Landing in England, they were met by no less than George Fox.[2] First, he asked Simon Bradstreet, "Did you have a hand in putting to death those four servants of God, whom they hanged for being Quakers only?"

Simon Bradstreet had to confess that he did.

George Fox continued, "You have put them to death on your own will without any law."

This frightening accusation was followed by an introduction to a man who said he was the father of William Robinson and was interested in looking into the possibilities of an investigation of the Bay Colony concerning the death of his son. There were those who said the Commission should be held personally responsible. Simon Bradstreet was growing more and more concerned, as he had already admitted his participation.

Simon Bradstreet and John Norton nervously looked around to see who were those other people approaching the dock to meet them. They were momentarily reassured to see two young men with their hats removed. At last some respect was being shown to those visiting dignitaries. When the two hatless men came closer, they recognized Christopher Holder and John Copeland. Their heads were not bared in respect, but in exhibition of the raw red marks around the holes in the righthand side of their heads, indicating where their ears had been.

Simon Bradstreet and John Norton did not remain long in England, following such a chilly welcome. They boarded the first boat they could find returning to Boston. John Norton wished he could die, and he did quite soon after they landed in Boston. Anne Bradstreet had expected a hero's return. It was not her first disappointment.[3]

Governor Endicott was in a difficult predicament. He knew he could not afford to displease King Charles II any more, as the original Massachusetts Bay Colony Charter could easily be withdrawn. If Endicott followed the request of Charles II to send any Quakers back to England for trial, he was sure the "cursed sect" would ruin him with their "tall tales." On the other hand, Endicott could not stand having the Quakers remain in Boston.

There were still many Quakers in Massachusetts Bay Colony in 1661, more in Salem than in Boston, and many were women. The Puritan women were becoming more and more distraught by the obsessive cruelty of the domineering men. Some had the courage to seek solace secretly by joining the Quaker meetings. By so doing, they escalated rather than escaped the cruelty.

Richard Bellingham was chosen as the best man to help clear Massachusetts of the dreaded Quakers. He and the magistrates invented a new law that surpassed all others for creative cruelty.

"The Cart and Tail Law" was passed by the Boston magistrates in 1661.[4] As the name of the law did not indicate that the objects for punishment were Quakers, the Boston magistrates hoped that it would not draw the attention of the English. The law provided that any Quaker found in Boston should be stripped to the waist and fastened to the tail of a cart and beaten as he or she was dragged along behind the moving vehicle. They would be driven from Boston to the next town where the local sergeant would arrange for similar transportation to the following town. These Quakers would thus be whipped half-naked from town to town until they were out of the jurisdiction of Massachusetts Bay Colony.

The magistrates were not slow to implement the law. People along the roadside would stop to watch with horrified wonder at these forsaken creatures, half-naked to the world, limping with bleeding feet, stretching with arms yanked into submission, cringing as the whips cracked across their mutilated backs. Many of the elderly victims did not survive. From Boston to Roxbury to Dedham to Providence they would be dragged until at last their battered remains could be set free outside of Massachusetts. This treatment of Quakers continued until the death of Endicott, the instigator of "The Cart and Tail Law," in 1665. At that time, the General Court of Massachusetts was commanded by a Royal Commission to remove all disabilities for Quakers, but whippings continued until 1677. It was partly the great distance from England which protected the administrators of the Cart and Tail Law from the scrutiny of the mother country. The death penalty was formally repealed in 1681. It was a gradual realization, but Mary had the last word and her sacrifice was vindicated, for in the end the Puritans paid a heavy price. Although Quakers continued to be arrested for preaching in Boston until 1672, the Royal Charter was withdrawn in 1686, and the settlers lost their title to the land, while a British governor assumed rule of the colony. He established an Anglican Church in Boston, which pulled the rug out from under the Puritans. Even so, Massachusetts was so determined that their Puritan tradition should survive, for it did not separate church from state until 1833; it was the last of the states to do so.

The uncompromising Puritans had, however, unconsciously contributed much encouragement to the cause they detested. Those who supported the cause of tolerance became strengthened, sharpened, and more vehement in their pursuit of religious freedom because of the tenacity of the Puritan leaders.

23. Portrait said to be of John Clarke by Guillaume
de Ville (courtesy of Redwood Library and Athenaeum,
Newport, RI).

{ 27 }
John Clarke in London

When John Clarke left Newport in 1651 with William Dyer and Roger Williams, he had no idea that he and his wife, Elizabeth, would remain in London for the next thirteen years. One of the many advantages of returning to London was the availability of the printing press. There, one could circulate one's thoughts in printed form, and a well-considered treatise presented to Parliament could change history.

John Clarke took this opportunity by writing several treatises to be circulated in Parliament emphasizing the aging despotism of Massachusetts Bay Colony in contrast to the growing liberalism in England, which he exposed in Ill News From New England by saying, "While Old England is being New, New England is becoming Old." John Clarke urged the recognition of the rights of Rhode Island as the up and coming colony. This treatise was signed by John Clarke, not as lawyer, nor minister, but "physician of Rhode Island in America."[1] Although Cromwell was interested in Rhode Island as a distant investment, he was very distracted by his intense desire to destroy the Roman Catholics in Ireland, along with all their mighty castles and cathedrals.

The cost of publishing as well as other expenses were high and John Clarke must now try to manage in London. He missed the produce of his farm in Newport, and his London practice of medicine did not bring in sufficient income to take care of all his needs.

In the meantime, the people of Rhode Island were beginning to wonder about John Clarke. How many more years did he need to accomplish his mission to procure the desired charter for Rhode Island? Was he skylarking in London? Roger Williams wrote a letter suggesting that they send William Dyer and John Greene over to London to take over the assignment of getting the charter.[2] It was the year after Mary's death and William felt proud to be chosen for such an important mission by the Colony. Although he had been politically inexperienced when he left England as a milliner, every year he had continued to step higher and higher in the affairs of the Colony. Just when he was preparing to leave, a letter arrived from John Clarke saying "Our affaire is in a forward way to be effected there to the great comfort of the Colony, and ... moneys only be waiting to manadge the matter." This letter gave Benedict Arnold a second thought, and he went to consult with William Dyer. They decided to take John Clarke at his word and do their best to raise the necessary money to help him.

Benedict Arnold and William Dyer concocted a plan together for raising the necessary funds, in a way that the sum would be divided proportionately between Newport, Portsmouth, and Warwick.[3] It was decided that agreed amounts could be paid in beef, pork, corn, peas, or other commodities at the going market rate, with allowances for certain persons who could not pay the rate until the corn was ripe and saleable or the "cattell be fitt to kill." It was decided that Newport would raise 129 pounds. Portsmouth 55 pounds and ten shillings, Providence 55 pounds and ten shillings, and Warwick 48 pounds. It was hard to gather the desired sum.

Commissioner William Dyer worked night and day arranging for the collection of available goods to get the amount needed to obtain a satisfactory charter. As William went from farm to farm, his mourning for his wife was eased by the realization that he was furthering the cause which Mary died for. It took imagination to convince the farmers that they should contribute to Clarke's work, the need for which was not clear to all. William Dyer was eloquent in explaining to each farmer how his corn would finance freedom for Rhode Island. It was an early example of taxation of the individual for the common good. When the money finally arrived in London, John Clarke knew that it represented loving toil, and continued faith in his mission, and he felt heartened to realize that he had not been forgotten during his long absence from Rhode Island.

The beginning of the reign of King Charles II in 1660 was burdened by the memory of his father's execution in 1649 and the new King feared assassination. He put some of John Clarke's good friends on trial. Sir Oliver Cromwell was one of the first to be put to death, and blind John Milton had to go into hiding. Sir Harry Vane had favored rule by the people instead of the monarchy, but he had been utterly opposed to the execution of Charles I. When the plot to kill the king was being planned, Sir Harry left Parliament to avoid involvement. King Charles II betrayed his promise, made at Breda, that all who did not have a part in the slaying of his father would be pardoned when he returned to England, and imprisoned Sir Harry.

The snow was falling in London in 1662, as a sleigh stood ready to transport Sir Harry Vane from prison to gallows. Dressed in a scarlet vest, he waved back to all his supporters leaning out of their windows and calling passionately to him. John Clarke was the only friend from Rhode Island present, to pay a last farewell to the man who had been "the sheet anchor of Rhode Island" in London.

The next day Samuel Pepys wrote in his diary that the decision to execute Sir Harry Vane was the worst mistake ever made by Charles II. "It will take him years to outlive it," wrote Pepys.

John Clarke knew that he could not take years to forgive the King, if John was to fulfill his mission for Rhode Island. He would have to substitute criticism for praise. With a physician's eye, it was time to study the personality of Charles II, who kept a busy schedule. Each morning, the king arose at 5 a.m. to start his nineteen-hour day. His harried council would scramble for early appointments only to discover that the King was hunting in Epping Forest or rowing on the Thames. He had a great love of the sea, and his favorite coronation present was his yacht from the Dutch. "Jag" meant "to chase" in Dutch. For years, these fast, slender Jachtships had been used to chase pirates. He thought it would be fun to chase his brother James up the Thames, so he had a sister yacht built for him. Charles and James found great sport in racing each other around the Isle of Wight. In so doing, King Charles introduced yacht racing for pleasure to England. He was also an expert court tennis player. Members of his council could often track him down on the tennis court for a little business. He liked music at his meals and plays by John Dryden after lunch.

There were plenty of pretty girls around the palace to dance with in the evening. There was no accurate account of the number of mistresses or illegitimate children. Catherine Braganza of Portugal, eventually became his barren queen.

However, sports and entertainment were not Charles' only interests. The most passionate was science. He concocted experiments for every aspect of his world. He had sturgeons transported to a fresh water pond in St. James park to see if they would survive. Wanting to know what the inside of a human being was like, he had his own private laboratory complete with cadavers for dissection. In his privy garden, he had a sun dial and an astronomical telescope referred to as the "King's Tube."

The scientific curiosity of this lively King was contagious. In 1662 he founded the Royal Academy with members from different religions, countries, and professions. This policy was not arrived at in a spirit of benevolence so much as a realization that one could not be exclusive in the search for a "Philosophy of Mankind." The Royal Society wanted to attract the best scientific minds to work and think "in company" without fear of violence.

Scientific inquiry was in the air. John Clarke saw the possibility of packaging science and religion into his request for a charter. He had diagnosed the King, and now the "physician from Rhode Island" would prescribe a most unusual lively experiment to His Majesty.

{ 28 }
The "Livelie" Experiment

After two years of courting King Charles II, John Clarke felt the time had come to approach him and tell him of the opportunities in Rhode Island. On January 28, 1662, he brought the king his first request for a Royal Charter. It began with a description of the adventures of the first settlers of Rhode Island, telling how they had

> quit their dear, native country and their near and precious relatives and enjoyments therein. To expose themselves and their families to all the hazards and inconveniences which they might meet on the vast and swelling ocean over which they should pass, or in the barbarous and howling wilderness to which they might come ... After a long encounter with many perils of sea and robbers [they] arrived ... in America where for the ... causes of conscience, and for peace sake, they were also necessitated to travail further among the barbarians in places untrod and with no small hazard, to seek out a place of habitation ... Where they might in freedom of conscience worship the Lord their God, as they were persuaded ... in this vast and desolate wilderness ... the natives quit their land to make room for the Colonists. They purchased, possessed and planted those parts of the world in all desirable freedom and liberty in all respects tried to keep laws as close as possible to England ...[1]

Never forgetting his salutes to the King, John Clarke reassured him that "Under the wing of your royal protection we went to flourish ... with permission for freedom of conscience as they are persuaded to pray for the life of the King. Live forever."

The next day, he delivered the letter to Buckingham Palace. As the letter remained unanswered, John Clarke had the feeling that maybe he had circled around the King. Undaunted, he wrote a second petition on February 5, 1662, this time going straight to the point, presenting his request as one which would hold double benefits for the King and for Rhode Island:

> To Charles the second:
> By the wonderful, provident, and gratious disposing of the Most High, of England, Scotland, and Ireland, with large dominions and territoryes thereto belonging, High and Mighty King:
> The humble petition and representation of John Clarke on the behalf and in the names of the purchasers and free in habitants of Rhode Island, and the rest of the Colony of Providence Plantations, in the Narragansett Bay in New England ...

The Charter started out by presenting Rhode Island as a good, safe, and most profitable investment for England. After introducing the soundness of the investment, John Clarke went on to suggest the adventure. The crucial statement was on freedom of religion. John Clarke wrote:

> That it is much on their hearts, if they be permitted, to hold forth a Livelie Experiment, that a most flourishing Civil State may stand and best be maintained, and that among our English subjects, with a full liberty in religious concernments, and that true Piety, rightly ground upon Gospel Principles, will give the best and greatest Security to Sovereignty and will lay in the hearts of men the strongest Obligations to true Loyalty.[2]

The Charter is conspicuously addressed towards men. However, it in no way insinuates Roger Williams' attitude that women are unregenerate and considered to be the "weaker vessel" in God's ultimate design. Nor does it suggest with George Fox the unique sensitivities of women which need expression to complement men's search for the truth. Presumably, women are included as "persons" in the most important clause of the Charter, which states:

> ... no Person within the said Colony, at any Time hereafter, shall be in any wise molested, punished, disquieted or called in Question for any Difference in Opinion in Matters of Religion, [which] do not actually disturb the peace of our colony ...

After having waited out the Winter of 1662 hoping for a response from the King, John Clarke was permitted an audience in response to his two petitions in the Spring of 1663. It was his best chance to persuade King Charles II that this venture across the Atlantic would be the most lively of any of his experiments. John Clarke had captured the imagination and confidence of King Charles II, who became an enthusiastic supporter of the Rhode Island "experiments."

Observing that although the King was quick to respond to new ideas, he abhorred paper work, John Clarke suggested that he would be happy to help the King by writing the Charter for him.[3] King Charles was delighted.

John Clarke not only incorporated the ideas of the petitions into the Charter, but he seized the opportunity to slip in a host of other benefits for Rhode Island. It was the only charter ever granted by Great Britain which was composed by the recipient. His Majesty's officers of state hoped to read the Charter before the final signing and sealing, "but fearing the lion's roaring they couched, against their wills to his Majesty's pleasure." Parliament had no authority over foreign affairs. That responsibility was left in the hands of the King and his advisors, and on July 9, 1663, the Rhode Island Charter received the royal signature "By the King Howard."

The Charter was made out in the name of the twenty-five Rhode Island magistrates. Of those, eight men had signed the Portsmouth Compact in Coddington's brick house in Boston twenty-five years ago. They were: John Clarke, William Brenton, William Coddington, William Baulston, John Porter, Samuel Wilbore, Randall Holden, and William Dyer. For twenty-five years, these men had stayed bonded together with hope. William Dyer was the closest to John Clarke. Together, they had surveyed the island of Aquidneck. Together, they had codified the first laws of 1644-1647. John Clarke looked forward to returning to his working companionship in Newport. He would need the assistance of William Dyer in codifying the laws suggested by this charter of 1663.

John Clarke was ecstatic in the culmination of his thirteen years of waiting in London for this golden opportunity. He had a few affairs to settle before the anticipated return to Rhode Island. The next important business was to find the quickest possible transportation for the prize news. The treasure was packed in a golden chest. Captain George Baxter had a vessel ready to transport it to Newport.

{ 29 }
Newport 1663

On the eve of November 26, 1663, Captain George Baxter landed in Newport, carrying his treasure in the golden box. The residents of Rhode Island were gathered around bonfires in the town square. And, when Governor Benedict Arnold opened the golden box, the crowd pressed close in order to catch a glimpse of the large roll of parchment resting inside the box. There was so much wild shouting and laughter that the sentinels had to blow their trumpets to maintain order. More cheers were heard when the great seal of King Charles II was broken and six feet of parchment were unrolled. A table was secured for Captain Baxter to stand above the crowd so that the Charter could be "held up on high and presented to the perfect view of all the people." With a voice that rolled like the ocean surf, Captain Baxter slowly read the contents of the Charter to the spellbound gathering.

Many vital subjects were addressed, but one line shone out above all others. It gave to every man the right to choose his own form of religious worship without interference or punishment from the State. The words sounded like magic in response to the long-standing prayers and petitions of the assembled group. For twenty-eight years the people of Rhode Island had suffered physical torture, prison, exile, and even hangings as punishments for differing with the dictates of the Puritans of Massachusetts Bay Colony. Each man straightened with pride as his name was read out as petitioner for the Charter and receiver of the same. This was the first document in America, and possibly Europe, to legalize freedom of religion.

There was too much to comprehend in one reading. The Charter would have to be read over and over again. Although the words were simple, they carried the emotion of poetry and the ecstasy of song. The people of Rhode Island knew that this was the culmination of the thirteen years that John Clarke had spent in London. They had to celebrate without him. He was detained settling his affairs in London and would be trailing his prize in a few months. When Clarke returned, they would take out the Charter to hear it read once more. They became so enamored of the ceremony that it became a yearly custom to reread their Charter for the public in celebration of its anniversary.

The night of the first reading, William Dyer returned to his home around midnight brimming with emotion. Although he had a new family — he had married Catherine the year before and they had a new daughter, Elizabeth — it was Mary he felt closest to that night. Their marriage had been stormy at times. But this night, it was different. William Dyer's tears fell with the ease of snowflakes floating in patterns of relief, etched in individuality, soft, beautiful, rising, and falling. In the whirl of small patterns, he began to see a larger design. He thought of Mary and her baffling spirituality. He thought of himself and his uncompromising practicality. It suddenly occurred to him that there had been a victory in the rocky marriage of Mary and William Dyer. They had both dedicated their lives in different ways to freedom of religion. For the first time, he felt a sense of peace in that final sublime unity which had, in the end, overcome the pain of their separation. Mary had sacrificed her life in the pursuit of freedom of religion which they both had sought. William still had some life left. He could hardly wait for John Clarke to return from England so that they could start working together codifying the laws made possible by the Charter.

The Charter was not changed for 181 years. Each year, the people of Rhode Island gathered together to be reminded of its contents. One hundred twenty-eight years later, its influence was discernable in the Bill of Rights (December 15, 1791). It stated:

> Congress shall make no law respecting an establishment of religion, or prohibiting the free exercise thereof; or abridging the freedom of speech, or of the press; or the right of people

peaceably to assemble, and petition the Government for redress of grievances.

Mary Dyer was the only woman in America to die for her Quaker beliefs, and her death made her message audible and visible.

As one anonymous English author summarized the impact of her life:

"The most important fact concerning Mary Dyer is that her murder having been the motive of the wonderfully liberal Charter granted by Charles II to the province of Rhode Island to make it the first spot of earth on the globe, whose religious toleration and absolute freedom of worship was set by law" — a statement which affirms Mary's own personal declaration when she wrote to Governor Endicott and the Boston magistrates:

My life not availeth me
In comparison to
The liberty of the Truth.

ENDNOTES

CHAPTER 1

1 De Croese, George, *History of the Quakers*, London, 1696.
2 Alice DuPont Ortiz made F.N. Dyer's report on family origins the subject of an address to the National Society of Colonial Dames in Delaware in 1938.

CHAPTER 2

1 Dyer, Cornelius, *Some Records of the Dyer Family*, Thomas Whittaker, 2+3 Bible House, New York, N.Y., 1994, p. 128.
2 The bodkin is owned by Kip Kelso Boden of Wilmington, Delaware, a descendant of the Dyers' second son William.
3 American Genealogist, U. 20 p. 186, U. 26, p. 229, U. 27, p. 216.
4 Dyer, Louis, William Dyer, *A Somerset Royalist in England,* Sudbury Ledge, 69 Banbury Road, Oxford, p. 3.

CHAPTER 3

1 Rutman, *Winthrop's Boston*, p.7-8, *Winthrop's Sermon* aboard the *Arabella*.
2 *Massachusetts Colony Records*, I, p.157, 181.
3 John Winthrop first landed in Salem and then made a temporary settlement in Charleston, where the water was so bad that half the group died the first winter from scurvy. Dudley persuaded Winthrop to settle in Newtowne (Cambridge), where he started to build a house. He was later invited by Blackstone (living alone on Shawmut Peninsula) to move to where there was good spring water. Winthrop dismantled his house in Newtowne and moved permanently to Boston.
4 Winthrop, John, *Journal* I, p. 176. Winthrop subscribed to the use

of land as a dividend for investment. No formal act of court deeded land to a specific individual.

5 The fear of fire was so great that a law was passed stating that: If any man should "wittingly or feloniously set on fire any dwelling house, store houses, or shall in like matter set on fire an out house, barn, stable, leans, stacks of hay, corn or wood, or anything of light nature" he shall be put in prison or to death. Ancient Charters, Acts Respecting Capital Crimes, ch. xviii.

6 A house was built at town expense for a herder. The Dyers paid five shillings a head for the privilege of incorporating their stock with the common herd on Romney Marsh where they were free to graze during the day and confined in a "payled yard" at night.

Boston residents were allowed to keep only one or two cows which were collected every morning from their homes before sunrise by the town herder, Richard Fairbank, taken to graze on Boston Commons, and returned to their owners at 6 p.m. in time for milking. For this service, the Dyers paid a bushel of corn a head to the herder.

7 *Massachusetts Colony Records*, Vol. 8, pp. 62-3.

All of the Boston residents (whether or not they were the privileged freemen) were expected to work on the Fort Hill project. Commissioners were chosen to "sette downe how many dayes work would be equal for each man to doe and what money they should contribute besides their work.

8 *Massachusetts Colony Records*, I, pp. 140-43, May, 1635.

9 Whitehall, Walter Muir, Boston, A Topographical History, p. 14.

10 Once a month, after the morning service, the non-members were asked to leave the church while the members remained for communion.

11 *Capitol Laws for Breaking Any of the Ten Commandments*. Taken from *Ancient Charters, Charters and General Laws*, The Colony and Province of Massachusetts Bay, collected from public records and ancient printed books. Chapter XVII, pp. 53-62.

Thou shall have no other gods before me.
"If any man after legal conviction shall have or worship any other god but the Lord God, he shall be put to death."
Thou shalt not make unto thee any graven images.

"If any man or woman "beawitch," that is hath consulteth with a familiar spirit, they shall be put to death."

Thou shalt not take the name of the Lord in vain.

If any man "shall wittingly and willingly presume to blaspheme the holy name of God, Father or Holy Ghost with direct express presumptions, or high-handed blasphemy, either by willful or obstinate denying the true God, or his creation..." he shall be put to death.

Remember the Sabbath Day to keep it holy.

If any man shall steal on the Lord's Day he shall have "one ear cut off" for the first, "the other ear cut off for the second offence" and be put to death for the third offence.

Honor they father and mother.

"If any child or children above 16 years old, and of sufficient understanding, shall curse or smite their natural father or mother, he or she shall be put to death, unless he can be sufficiently testified, that the parents have been very unchristianly negligent in the education of such children, and so provoked them by other cruel corrections, that they have been forced thereunto to preserve themselves from death or maiming."

Thou shalt not kill.

"If any man shall commit any willful murder upon premeditated malice, hatred or cruelty, not in a man's necessary and just defence, or by mere casualty against his will, he shall be put to death."

Thou shalt not commit adultery.

"If any person commit adultery with a married or espoused wife, the adulterer and the adulteress shall surely be put to death."

Thou shalt not steal.

"If any person shall commit burglary, by breaking up any dwelling house, or shall rob any person in the field or highways, such person so offending, shall be for the first offence, be branded on the forehead with the letter (B)" ' 2nd time 'branded as before and severely whipped' ' 3rd time, 'he shall be put to death as being incorrigible.'

Thou shalt not bear false witness against thy neighbor.

'If any man rise up false witness wittingly, and of purpose to take a man's life ... he shall be put to death.'

Thou shalt not covet thy neighbour's house, wife, servant, ox, ass or anything.

'If a man shall ravish any maid or single woman committing carnal copulation, with her by force, against her own will, that is above the age of ten, he shall be put to death.'

12 Rutman's, *Winthrop*, p. 7-8

CHAPTER 4

1 Winthrop, *Journal* I, p. 53. 'Whereas Mr. Williams had refused to join with the congregation of Boston, because they would not make a public declaration of the irrepentance for having communion with the churches of England while they lived there' ...

2 Winthrop, *Journal* I, p. 157. 'Governor and assistants sent for Roger Williams, the occasion was for that he had taught publicly, that a magistrate ought not to tender an oath to an unregenerate man, for that we thereby have communion with a wicked man.'

3 Thomas Hooker was a minster of the Church of Newtowne (Cambridge) 1633-36. He joined John Haynes in Hartford, Connecticut in 1636, where he served as minister for the Hartford Church until his death in 1647.

4 *Massachusetts Colonial Records*, I, p. 160.

CHAPTER 5

1 Winthrop, *Journal* I, p. 170.

Here came Mr. Henry Vane, son and heir of Sir Harry Vane, comptroller of the King's house, who being a young gentleman of excellent parts, and has been employed by his father (when he was ambassador) in foreign affairs, forsook the honours and preferments of the Court, to enjoy the ordinance of Christ in their purity here.

2 Winthrop, *Journal* I (Hosmer) p.206

3 Piercy, Josephine K., *Anne Bradstreet*.

4 Winthrop, *Journal* I, p. 219.

Thus every occasion increased the contention, and caused great alienation of minds and the members of Boston ... did make much disturbance by public questions, and objections to their doctrines, which did any way disagree from their opinions, and so it began to be common here to distinguish between men, being under a covenant of grace or a covenant of works, as in other countries between Protestants and papists.

Winthrop, *Journal* I, p. 216-217.

Except men of good understanding and such as knew the bottom of their tenets of those of the party, few could see where the difference was.

5 John Wheelwright *Papers*, edited by Charles H. Bell, Prince So. Boston, 1876, p. 160-61.

6 The majority of Boston inhabitants were for Vane, but the outlying towns voted for Winthrop.

CHAPTER 6

1 Under the circumstances, it might appear strange that there seemed to be fewer maternal deaths among those women delivered by mid-wives, than others delivered by physicians. It was not until two centuries later that septicemia was diagnosed as one of the major causes of maternal death, transmitted by the unsterilized hands of the physicians, who alone felt qualified for internal examinations of the mother. The mid-wives were not considered adequately "trained" to reach inside the mother's womb.

CHAPTER 7

1 Winthrop, *Journal* I, p. 255.

2 William Dyer, with ten other men, built the dock to accommodate the residents of Charlestown commuting to the Boston Church.

3 Winthrop, *Journal* I, Vol. 1, p. 238. "In this time with great dangers with the Indians ' no person shall travel above one mile from his dwelling house, except in place where other houses are near together, without some arms, upon pain of twelve pence for every default."

4 The Meeting House in Newtowne was located on the corner of Spring and Water Streets (today, Mt. Auburn and Dunster Streets, Cambridge).

5 *Massachusetts Colonial Records*, Vol. I, pp. 201-208.

6 Ibid., p. 12.

7 Ibid., p. 14.

8 *Corinthians* 14:34-5:

> Women should keep silence in the church. For they are not permitted to speak, but should be subordinate as ever the law says ... If there is anything they desire to know, let them ask their husbands at home. For it is shameful for women to speak in church.
>
> *Timothy*: 2:12,
>
> Let a woman learn in silence with all submissiveness. I permit no woman to teach or have authority over men; she is to keep silent ... For Adam was formed first, then Eve.
>
> *St. Paul,*
>
> I permit no women to teach or have authority over men.

9 *Letters of Paul to Corinthians,*

> Aquila and Priscilla took it upon themselves to instruct Apollos ... Priscilla and Aquila salute the Lord with the church that is within their home.

10 Winthrop, *Short Story'Antinomian Controversy*, p. 248; Hutchinson, History: *The Examination of Mrs. Hutchinson*, pp. 366-368.

11 Winthrop, *Journal* (Hosmer), p.241. Ironically, this also meant that they could not travel more than one mile away without violating the law against traveling without firearms.

CHAPTER 8

1 *Massachusetts Historical Society Proceeding*, 2, Series 4, pp. 161-63, 190-91, The Church proceedings of the trial of Anne Hutchinson are reported by Ezra Stiles from shorthand notes of Robert Keaynes, New England, 1638.

2 Of all of the Antinomians banished from Boston, the only ones to be formally excommunicated from the Boston Church were Anne

Hutchinson, William Aspinwall, and John Wheelwright.

3 The "monster birth" is described in Winthrop, *History* I, p. 226.

4 A large number of the Boston Church attempted retaliation against Governor Winthrop but the Church elders would have none of it. Winthrop was not without scruples over the position he had taken. In his private journal he confessed:

> The great questions that have troubled the country are about the authority of the magistrates and the liberty of the people. It is yourselves that have called us to this office and being called by yore, we have our authority from God, in way of an ordinance, such as hath the image of God eminently stamped upon it. The contempt and violation whereof hath been vindicated with examples of divine vengeance.

5 Letter from Roger Williams to John Winthrop, 16/4/38.

CHAPTER 9

1 Clarke, John, Ill *News from New England.*

2 Ibid.

3 Joy-Dyer, Cornelia. *Some Records of the Dyer Family*, pp. 12- 13.

4 Clarke, John, Ill *News from New England.*

5 Chapin, Howard, *Documentary History of Rhode Island*, pp. 72-73.

6 Ibid., p. 94.

7 Dyer Island has submerged like a diving whale into the depths of Narragansett Bay and is now hardly one hundredth of its original size.

CHAPTER 10

1 All the meetings and laws are reported in the *Records of the Colony of Rhode Island.*

2 The problem of wolves continued and the Newport records of 1642 report that every man who could deliver the head of a wolf to the Meeting House would be rewarded with five pounds.

3 Contemprary references to the earthquake:

Newbury Town Record:

Wonders were revealed when the earthquake 'shook the earth ' in a very sudden violent manner to our great amazement and wonder. Men working in the fields cast down their working tools and ran 'with greatly terrified lookes, to the next company they could meet with.

Winthrop, *History I,* June 1, 1638, p. 318:

Between three and four in the afternoon, being clear, warm weather, the wind westerly, there was a great earthquake. It came with a noise like a continued thunder, and the rattling of coaches in London, but was presently gone ' It shook the ships that lay in the harbor and all the islands ' The noise and the shaking continued for four minutes. The earth was unquiet twenty days after.

4 Winthrop's *Journal* I, (Hosmer) p.277.

5 Hall, *Worlds of Wonder*, p.75

Strictly speaking, a wonder was distinct from a miracle, though in every day discourse, and even among the ministry, the two words became interchangeable.

6 Easton, *Journal.*

7 *Records of the Colony of Rhode Island*, May 30, 1638.

Everyman's allotment to be recorded in book shall be sufficient evidence for him and his rightly to possess and enjoy.

CHAPTER 11

1 Jefferys, CPB. *Newport, An Historical Sketch.*

2 All the Newport meetings are reported in Records of Colony of Rhode Island and Providence Plantations I, signed by William Dyre, Clerk, p. 87-128.

3 Chapin, Howard, *Documentary History of Rhode Island* II, p. 75.

4 Ibid., p. 74.

5 Williams, Roger, *Key to the Language of America.*

6 Brandenbaugh, *Fat Mutton and Liberty of Conscience*, pp. 28-36.

7 Chapin, Howard, *Documentary History of Rhode Island*, pp. 101-02.

8 Ibid., p. 93-106.

CHAPTER 13

1 Records of the Settlement for Providence, Portsmouth, and Warwick, 1637-1647, transcribed by John Russell Bartlett, Crawford Green, Providence, 1856.

2 Arnold, *History of the State of Rhode Island*, 1858, Comments:

We hazard little in saying that the digest of 1647, for simplicity of diction, unencumbered as it is by the superfluous verbiage that clothes our modern statutes in learned obscurity for breadth of comprehension, embracing as it does the foundation of the whole body of law, on every subject, which has since been adopted; and for vigor and originality of thought, and boldness of expression, and the brilliant triumph of the principle it embodies, presents a model of legislation which has never been surpassed.

CHAPTER 14

1 Winthrop, *Journal* I (Hosmer) p.92.

2 Clarke, Ill *News from New England*, p. 38

3 *Massachusetts Colonial Records* II, p. 85.

4 Clarke, Ill *News from New England*.

5 Winthrop, *Journal* I, p. 162.

Roger Williams preached that a man ought not to pray with an unregenerate man, though such be wife or child.

Hubbard, *General History of New England*, pp. 206-207.

He maintained that it is not lawful for an unregenerate man to pray, nor to take an oath, nor was it lawful for a godly man to have any communion either in family prayer, with such as they judged unregenerate.

Morton, Nathaniel, *New England Memorial*, p. 153:

He withdrew all private religious communion with the Church there (Salem) insomuch as he would not pray nor give thanks at meals with his own wife, because they went to the Church assemblies.

6 Mather, *Magnolia,* b. VII, Chapter 11, 6.

7 Williams, Roger, *George Fox digg'd out of his Burrow*, p. 361.

CHAPTER 15

1 There is no available record of what happened to the six children during the time both parents were in England. It was customary in the seventeenth century to board out children with another family. Otherwise, they might have stayed on the Dyer farm with the tenant farmer and his family.

CHAPTER 16

1 To Friends and Neighbors of Providence Written at Sir Henry Vane's at Belleau in Lincolnshire, April 1653

I hope it may have pleased the Most High Lord of sea and land to bring Captain Christen's ship and dear Mr. Dyre unto you and with him the Council's letters which answer the petition of Sir Harry Vane and myself, granted us, for the conformation of the Charter, until the determination of controversy. The determination is hindered by two main obstructions, the first is the mighty war with the Dutch, which makes England and Holland and the nations tremble. This hath made the Parliament set Sir Harry Vane and two or three more commissioners to manage the war, which they have done with much engaging the name of God with them, who hath appeared helping 60 of ours against almost 300 of their men of war, and perchance to the sinking and taking about 100 of theirs. The second obstruction is the opposition of our adversaries Arthur Haseling and Colonel Fenwicks. Under God, the sheer anchor of our ship is Sir Henry, who will do as the eye of God leads him, and he faithfully promised me that he would observe the motion of our New England business while I staid some ten weeks with his lady in Lincolnshire. Some of our friends think another Parliament will more favor us than this.

From Roger Williams.

2 *Records of Colony of Rhode Island and Providence Plantation I,* p. 243.

Whereas, there is a common cause practiced amongst Englishmen to buy negers, to that end they may have them for service or slaves forever; for the preventinge of such pratices among us, let it be ordered that no blacke mankind or white be forced by covenant bond, or otherwise, to serve any man or his assighness longer than ten years, or until he come bee twenty-four years of age, if they be taken in under fourteen, from the time of their comings within the liberties of this Collonie. And at the end of terme of ten years to sett them free.

3 Ibid, p. 243. Privateers were commanders of privately owned and manned armed vessels, commissioned by the government in time of war to fight the enemy, used especially for commercial shipping, compared to pirates who either robbed or committed illegal violence at sea or on the shores of the sea.

4 Ibid, p. 266. *La Fantasie*, The Correspondence of Roger Williams, p. 399.

5 Ibid., p. 389.

6 The Toro Synagogue stands today on its original location in Newport.

CHAPTER 17

1 Fox, George, *Journal*, p. 37.
Justice Bennet of Darby (who) was the first that called us Quakers, because I bid them tremble at the word of God. And this was in the year 1650." ("Quakers" prefer to be called "Friends.")

2 Spence MSS II, 135

3 Fox, Margaret, *A Brief Collection of Remarkable Passages*,

4 Swarthmore MSS

5 Fox, George, Journal

CHAPTER 19

1 The original Woodhouse Log is in the Morgan Library, New York City.

2 Anti-Quaker Laws in New Haven.
Every Quaker that came into the Jurisdiction should be severly whipt, and should be kept at the work in the House of Correction, and the second time, be branded in one hand, and kept at work as aforsaid, the third time, to be branded in the other hand, and the fourth time, to be bored through the tongue with a red hot iron."

3 Besse, *A Collection of the Sufferings of the Quakers*, Vol. II, p. 196.

4 Selleck, *Quakers in Boston*. After the minister had finished, it was a commonly accepted practice for the men in the congregation to rise and speak. Since attendance at all church services was compulsory, the occasion provided the quakers with a captive audience.

5 Braithwaite, The Beginnings of Quakerism. Holder, *Quakers in England and America*, p. 414.

6 Ibid.

CHAPTER 20

1 *Ancient Charters, Charters and General Laws of the Colony and Province of Massachusetts Bay*. Laws against Quakers, pp. 121-25.

2 Holder, *Quakers in England and America*, p. 243.

3 Ibid., p. 425.

CHAPTER 21

1 One hundred and twenty-five copies of the two letters, written by William Dyer to the Boston Magistrates were printed for Charles Dyer B. Norton and Daniel B. Dyer by the University Press, Cambridge, USA.

2 In the *Introduction to the Language of Native Americans*, Roger Williams describes how the Indians served as speedy postmen helping the English to communicate with one another. "It is admiral to see what paths their naked hardened feet have made in the wilderness in most stony and rocky places. They are generally quick on foot, brought up from the breasts to running, their legs being also from the womb stretched and bound up in a strange way on the cradle backward. Many of them run ... a hundred miles in a Summer day, and back within two days."

CHAPTER 22

1 The details of the trials and hangings are taken from the following records:

Besse, Joseph. *A Collection of Sufferings of People Called Quakers*, London, 1753 (taken from original records and authentic accounts).

Bishop, George. *New England Judged by the Spirit of the Lord*, London, 1803.

de Croese, George. *History of the Quakers*, London, 1696.

Hutchinson, Governor Thomas. *History of the Colony and Province of Massachusetts,* Vol. I, pp. 180-90.

Massachusetts Colonial Records, Vol. IV, Part 1, pp. 3-7, 17-19.

Roger Horatio, *Mary Dyer of Rhode Island, the Quaker Martyr that Was Hanged on Boston Commons*, Preston Round, Providence, RI, 1896.

Sewell, William. *A History of the Quakers*, 1799-80.

Stevenson, Marmaduke, *A Call From Life to Death*, Augerville Papers, Mensies Catalogue, No. 1, 903, London, 1660.

2 Bishop, George, *New England Judged by the Spirit of the Lord,* p. 288.

3 *Massachusetts Colonial Records* IV, Part I, p. 355.

4 Bishop, p. 311

CHAPTER 23

1 Although Shelter Island by its location is indeed a haven from storms at sea, the name was chosen for a place of protection for dissident religions from the Puritan autocracy.

2 There was constant trade between Rhode Island, Barbados, and the Azores, Rhode Island exporting horses, sheep, hogs, corn and importing wine, sugar. Will is the one of the Dyer children of whom we know the most. In 1664, when New Amsterdam became New York, he was appointed. Master of Customs, by King James. Later, Will was to become the seventh mayor of New York. He later moved to Maryland, where he has many descendants.

3 Roger Williams' letter to General Court of Massachusetts, 5/10/1654.

> At my last departure from England was importuned by the Narraganset Sachems ' to present their petition to the high Sachem of England [Cromwell] that they might not be forced from their religion, and for not changing their religion, be invaded by war, for they said they were daily visited with threatenings by Indians ' from ' Massachusetts, that if they would not pray, they would be destroyed by war.

4 Roger Williams to John Winthrop, 2/28/1637

I find what I could never hear before, that [the Indians] have plenty of Gods or divine powers: the Sun, Moon, Fire, Water, Snow, Earth, the Deer, the Bear, etc. are divine powers. I brought home lately from Narragansett the names of 38 other Gods ' but I hope that the time is not long that some shall truly bless the God in Heaven.

5 Taylor, *Account of Some of the Labors, Exercises, Travels, and Perils by Sea and Land of John Taylor of York, London*, printed by J. Borole, Whitehead Court, Gracious Street, XDCCX.

6 This document was printed as a Broadside, bound up under the title of "Quakers," and placed in the Bodleian Library with the shelf reference "Wood 645."

7 Second letter from Mary Dyer to Boston Magistrates.

CHAPTER 24

1 Quakers had brought linen and winding sheets in preparation for Mary Dyer's dead body. She was reportedly buried on Boston Commons, but the location is not known.

CHAPTER 25

1 Whittier, *Journal of Margaret Smith.*

2 Anne Bradstreet's poem to 'My Dear and Loving Husband':
  If ever two were one, than surely we.
  If ever man were loved by wife then thee.
  If ever wife was happy in a man,
  Compare with me, ye women, if you can,
  I prize thy love more than the whole mines of gold '

3 The death records of Newport compare Mary Tyler's death to that of the martyred Mary, Queen of Scots. In another manuscript of the Rhode Island Historical Society, a woman who had been imprisoned in Boston at the time of the first hanging has an afterthought on the lack of guilt expressed by the Boston magistrates and ministers:
  It had been thought that there had been some remorse, sorrow or repentance in the people of New England, for what they had done in hanging the people called Quakers; for some of this after generation does not care to hear of it, neither would they be

blamed for what their fathers and predecessors have done. However, we find in a little book of late date by four priests of Boston in New England, namely James Allen, Joshua Moody, Samuel Willard, and Cotton Mather, who seem still to justify what they have done in hanging the said people for they say "They (were) not abused: But dealt justly with (as) they came purposely to undermine the civil government and to persuade the people to renounce it.

4 The original copy of Anne Coddington's letter is in the Westerly, RI Historical Society.

5 Fox, George, *Journal* (Penney). "And whey (she) was put to death (as) I was in prison at Lancaster I had a perfect sense of it as though it had been myself and as though ye halter had beene putt about my necke."

6 Swarthmore, Mss. IV, p. 109.

7 Tompkins, John and Fied, John. *Piety Promoted, Collection of Dying Sayings of the People Called Quakers,* Dublin, 1721.

8 Benton, Thomas, *Femmes D'Amerique*, Armand Colin Co., Paris, France.

9 Fox, George, Journal. Holder, Charles F., *Quakers in Great Britain and America,* p. 429-430.

CHAPTER 26

1 Bishop, *New England Judged. Holder, Quakers in England and America*, p. 428-430.

2 Fox, George, *Journal*, p. 6. Holder, Charles F., *Quakers in Great Britain and America,* p. 432.

3 Bishop, *New England Judged*, p. 11. Simon Bradstreet was "a man hardened in blood and a cruel persecutor".

4 Massachusetts Records IV, p. 23. Cart and Tail Law the same as Vagabond Act.

5. Often they were arrested for using the personal pronoun "Thee".

CHAPTER 27

1 *Records of the Colony of Rhode Island* I, p. 433-35.

2 Ibid, pp. 442-47.

"At a consultation held at Newport on Rhode Island in New England, according to order of the Colony, concerning the sending of our Agent or Agents to present our humble petition and Allegiance to the King's Majesty in England, we whose names are underwritten doe agree to request our well-beloved and worthy friend Mr. Wm Dyre of Newport and Mr. John Greene of Warwick to undertake this honorable service in the name and behalf of the whole Colony to confirm the liberties under the 1644 Parliamentary patent. Witness our names. William Brenton, William Baulston, Benedict Arnold, Roger Williams, John Porter."
3 Ibid, pp. 447-48.

CHAPTER 28
1 Clarke, John, *Ill News from New England.*
2 The words of John Clarke in the Charter of 1663 are chiseled in marble under the dome of the State House in Providence, Rhode Island:

> To hold forth a lively experiment
> That a most flourishing state may stand
> And best be maintained with full liberty
> In religious concernments.

3 The original Royal Charter of 1663 is on display at the State House in Providence, Rhode Island. It hangs outside the Senate room and may be seen by drawing red velvet curtains. A portrait of Charles II tops the document and merry-looking beavers swim up and down the margins, suggesting enterprises to be considered besides the lofty ideals.

BIBLIOGRAPHY

Adams, Brooks, *Emancipation of Massachusetts*, Houghton Mifflin, Boston, Mass., 1962.

Adams, Charles Francis, *Three Episodes in Massachusetts History*, Russell Research, New York, N.Y., 1965.

Adams, James Truslow, *Founding of New England*, Little Brown, 1921.

Alderman, Clifford Lindsay, *The Rhode Island Colony*, Crowell Collier Press, Collier MacMillan, London, 1969.

Allen, Rowland, H., *New England Tragedy in Prose, The Coming of the Quakers*, Nicholas Noyes, Boston, 1869.

Ancient Charters, Charters and General Laws of the Colony and Province of Massachusetts Bay Colony, T.B. Waite, Boston, 1812.

Anderson, Rev. James, *Memorable Women of Puritan Times*, Blackie & Son, London, 1866.

Arnold, Samuel Greene, *History of the State of Rhode Island*, D. Apple Co., New York, N.Y., 1859.

Ashley, Maurice, Charles II, *The Man and the Statesman,* Praeger, New York, N.Y., 1971.

Bacon, Margaret Hope, *As the Way Opens, The Story of Quaker Women in America*, Friends University Press, Richmond, Indiana, 1980.

Baltzell, Digby, *Puritan Boston and Quaker Philadelphia*, MacMillan, New York, N.Y., 1979.

Barbour, Hugh, *The Quaker in Puritan England*, Yale University Press, 1964.

Barber, Samuel, *Boston Commons*, Christopher Press, Boston, Mass., 1914.

Barclay, A.R., Letters of Early Friends, London, 1841.

Barker, Shirley, *Builders of New England*, Dodd Mead, New York, N.Y., 1965.

Barrows, C.E., *First Baptist Church in Newport*, Sanborn Printer, 1876.

Beals, Carlton, *Colonial Rhode Island*, Thomas Nelson, Inc., Camden, N.J., 1970.

Belloc, Hillaire, Charles II, *The Last Rally*, Harper & Bros., New

York/London, 1939.

_____, *Milton*, J.P. Lippincott, Philadelphia/London, 1935.

Benton, Thomas, *Femmes D'Amerique*, Armand Colin & Co., Paris, France.

Besse, Joseph, *A Collection of the Suffering of People Called Quaker* (taken from original records and authentic accounts), London, 1753. Franklin Books, Philadelphia, Pa.

Best, Mary Agnes, *Mary Dyer ' The Bloody Town of Boston*, Ruskin House, London.

Bicknell, Thomas W., *Story of Dr. John Clarke*, Providence, R.I., published by author, 1915.

_____, *History of the State of Rhode Island and Providence Plantations*, New York, N.Y., 1920.

Birkhead, Sarah, *Governor William Coddington* Bishop, George, *New England Judged by the Spirit of the Lord*, London, 1803, reprinted Thomas Strachney, Philadelphia, Penn.,1885.

Bohn, Ralph, *Controversy Between Puritans and Quakers*, Edinburg, 1955.

Bolton, Charles, *The Real Founders of New England*, F.W. Fakon, Boston, Mass., 1929.

Bowle, John, *Charles the First*, Little Brown, Boston, Mass., 1975.

Bradford, William, *Plymouth Plantation, 1620-1647*, Random House, 1981.

Braithwaite, William C., *The Beginning of Quakerism*, MacMillan, New York, N.Y., 1912.

Breene, T.H., *Puritans and Adventurers*, Oxford University Press, 1980.

Brenton, *History of Brenton Point*, Goodspeed Co., Boston, Mass., 1963.

Bridenbaugh, Carl, *Fat Mutton and Liberty of Conscience*, Brown University Press, Providence, R.I., 1974.

Bryant, Arthur, *King Charles II*, Longman Green & Co., London/New York/Toronto, 1931.

Bushman, Richard, *From Puritans to Yankees*, W.W. Norton, 1967.

Cadbury, Henry, *The Captain of Shelter Island*, Friends, March 20, 1653.

Cady, Jane Hutchins, *Rhode Island Boundaries*, 1636-1936, State Planning Board, Rhode Island and Providence Plantation, Rhode Island Tercentary Committee, 1936

Calvin, John, *Institutes of Christian Religion*, Geneva, 1618.

Chapin, Charles, *A History of Rhode Island Ferries*, 1640-1923, Oxford Press, Providence, R.I., 1925.

Chapin, Howard, *Documentary History of Rhode Island*, Preston & Round Co., Providence, R.I., 1919.

Clarke, John, *Ill News From England*, London, Henry Hills, 1652.

Cooper, Elizabeth, *Life and Letters of Lady Arabella Stuart*, Huret & Blackett, London, 1866.

Cotton, John, *The Way of Life*, London, 1641.

Covey, Cyclone, *The Gentle Radical*, Roger Williams, MacMillan, New York, 1966.

Crosfield, Helen G., *Margaret Fox of Swarthmore Hall*, LondonBishopgate, Headley Brothers, 1913.

De Croese, George, *History of Quakers*, London, 1696.

Dos Passos, *The Ground We Stand On*, Harcourt Brace, New York, N.Y., 1921.

Dow, George F., *Domestic Life In New England*, Perkins Press, 1923.

_____*Every Day Life In Massachusetts Bay Colony,* Society for the Preservation of New England Antiquities, 1935.

Downing, Antoinette, F., *Architectural Heritage of Newport*, 1640-1915.

Drake, Marjorie, *The Book of Boston,* Hastings House, New York, N.Y., 1960.

Drake, Samuel Adams, *Founders of New England.*

Duvall, Ralph G., *The History of Shelter Island*, 1652-1952, Shelter Island Heights, N.Y., 1952.

Dyer, Cornelia C. Joy, *Some Records of the Dyer Family*, Thomas Whitaker, N.Y., New York, N.Y., 1864.

Dyer, Lewis, William Dyer, *A Somerset Royalist in New England,* Oxford, Surbry Lodge, 1660.

Dyer, William Allen, *The Name Dyer*, Syracuse, N.Y., 1946.

Earle, Alice Morse, *Home Life in Colonial Days*, Berkshire Press, Stockbridge, Mass., 1974.

_____, *Customs and Fashions in Old New England*, Scribners, New York, 1874.

_____, *Women of Colonial and Revolutionary Times*, Scribners, New York, 1895.

Easton, Emily, *Roger Williams*, Houghton Mifflin, Riverside Press, Boston, Mass., 1930.

Easton, Nicholas, *Rhode Island Diary from Morton's New England Memories,* Cambridge, Mass., 1699.

Eastonas, Ralph M., *Some Famous Privateers of New England*, New York State Street Trust, 1928.

Ellis, George, *Puritan Age in Massachusetts*, Houghton Mifflin, Riverside Press, Boston, Mass., 1883.

Emmett, Elizabeth R., *The Story of Quakerism*, London/Bishopgate Street

Without, Headley Brothers, 1908.

Erikson, Kai, *Wayward Puritans*, John Wiley, New York, 1960.

Evans, Charles, *Friends in the 17th Century*, Friends Bookstore, Philadelphia, Penn., 1875.

Everett, Edward, *The Story of Massachusetts*, Russell and Russell, New York, N.Y., 1965.

Fells, Margaret, *A Brief Collection of Remarkable Passages and Occurrences Relating to Birth, Education Life, etc.*, S. Serole, Gracious St., London, 1710,

Field, John, *Collection of Dying Sayings of Many of the People Called Quakers*, Dublin, Ireland, 1721.

Founding of Massachusetts, *Sources of History of the Settlement, 1628-1631*. Massachusetts Historical Society, Boston, 1930.

Fowler, Robert, *Log of Woodhouse*, 1657.

Fox, George, *The Journal of George Fox,* Vols 1 & 2, edited from the manuscript by Norman Penney, University Press, Cambridge, John C. Winston Co., Philadelphia, 1911.

Fox, Margaret, *A Brief Collection of Remarkable Passages*, J. Sowle in White Hart Court in Gracious S. London, 1710.

Fraser, Antonio, *Cromwell the Lord Protector,* Alfred Knopf, 1973.

_____, Royal Charles, *Charles II and Restoration*, Alfred Knopf, 1979, 1979.

French, Allen, *Charles I and the Puritan Upheaval,* Houghton Mifflin, 1955.

Frost, J. William, *Quaker Family in Colonial America*, St. Martin's Press, New York, 1973.

Greene, George Washington, *A Short History of Rhode Island*, JA and RA Reid, 1877, Providence, R.I.

Grieve, Robert, *The Sea Trade in Rhode Island,* Providence, R.I., 1902.

Hailer, William, *Puritan Frontiers, 1630-1660.*

Hale, Edward Everett, *The Story of Massachusetts*, Lothrop Co., Boston, Mass., 1891.

Hall, David C., *The Antinomian Controversy*, 1638-38, A Documentary History, Wesleyan, 1968.

Hall, Warren, *Pagans, Puritans, Patriots of Yesterday's Southhold*, Historical Council, Cutchogue, N.Y., 1935

Hallowell, R.P., *Quaker Invasion of Massachusetts*, Houghton Mifflin, Boston, 1883.

_____, *Pioneers Quakers*, Boston, Riverside Press, 1987.

Hardy, Blanche Christobel, Arabella Stuart, E.P. Dutton, Co., New York, N.Y., 1913.

Heidish, Marcy Moran, *Witnesses*, Houghton Mifflin, 1887.

Hill, Christopher, *Milton and the English Revolution*, Faber & Faber, 3 Queen Street, London, 1977.

Holder, Charles Fred, *Quakers in Great Britain and America*, Newner & Company, New York/Los Angles/London, 1913.

Hodges, George, *The Hanging of Mary Dyer*, Moffet Yard & Company, N.Y., 1907.

Hosman, J.K., *Records of the Government of Massachusetts Bay in New England, 1630-1649*.

Hubbard, William, *A General History of New England*, Massachusetts Historical Society, Hillard and Metcalf, 1815.

Hutchinson, Governor Thomas, *History of the Colony and Province of Massachusetts Bay Colony*, edited by Laurence S. Mayo, Howard University Press, 1936.

Janney, Samuel M., *History of the Religious Society of Friends*, Hangs and Zell, Philadelphia, Penn., 1868.

Jefferys, C.P.B., *Newport 1639-1976*, An Historical Sketch, Newport Historical Society, 1970.

Jones, Rufus, *Quakers in American Colonies*, London, MacMillan, 1911.

_____, *The Story of George Fox*, MacMillan, 1919.

Josselyn, John, *An Account of Two Voyages to New England*, collection of the Massachusetts Historical Society, Vol. III, third series, 1833, pp. 211-354.

Ketty, Mary Ann, *Memories of the Primitive Lives and Persecution of the Quaker*, London, Harvey & Darton, 1887.

King, Basil, *The Hanging of Mary Dyer*, McClures, May-November 1902.

Knowles, James D., *Memoirs of Roger Williams*, Lincoln Edmunds & Co., Boston, Mass., 1834.

La Fantasie, *The Correspondence of Roger Williams*, 2 Vols., University Press of New England, 1988.

Lodge, Henry Cabot, *Boston, Longman* Greece, New York, N.Y., 1891.

Loth, David, *Royal Charles Ruler and Rake*, Brentano, New York, N.Y., 1930.

Massachusetts Colonial Records

Massey, George Valentine II, *Ancestry of Elizabeth*, Du Pont Bayord for her Children, 1953.

Mather, Cotton, *Magnalia Christi Americana*, T. Parkhust, London, 1702.

Mayo, Lawrence Shaw, *John Endicott,* Harvard University Press, 1936.

McCallum, Jane, *Women Pioneers*, Johnson Pub., Richmond, N.Y., 1929.

McLoughlin, William G., *Rhode Island*, W.W. Norton, New York, N.Y., 1978,

Miller, Perry & Johnson, Thomas. *A Sourcebook of the Writings of Puritans*, Harper & Row, 1938.

_____, *The New England Mind from Colony to Providence*, Beacon Press, Boston, Mass., 1953.

_____, *Errand in the Wilderness*, Harvard University Press, 1978.

_____, *Orthodoxy in Massachusetts*, 1630-1650, Peter Smith, Gloucester, Mass., 1965.

Mohr, Ralph S., *Rhode Island Governors for 300 Years*, Graves Registration, August 1954.

Morgan, Edmund, *The Puritan Dilemma*, The Story of John Winthrop, Little Brown, Boston, Mass., 1958.

Morison, Samuel Eliot, *Building of the Bay Colony*, Harghton Mayer, 1964.

Morton, Nathaniel, *New England Memorial*, Crocker and Brewster, Boston, 1820.

Nelson, Wilbur, *Ministry of John Clarke*, Newport, R.I., 1927.

_____, *Life of John Clarke*, Ward Printing Co., Newport, R.I., 1923.

_____, *Hero of Aquidneck*, Fleming & Rewell, Co., New York, N.Y., 1954.

New England Historical and Genealogical Register, January 1950, Register 98.

Newman, Daisy, *A Procession of Friends*, Friends United Press, Richmond, Ind., 1972.

Nobles, Bryant R., *An Investigation of the Political Theory on Dr. John Clarke's Writing,* Thesis M.A., Hardin Simmons University, 1969.

Notestan, Wallace, *The English People, 1603-1630 on the Eve of Colonization*, New York, N.Y.

Palfrey, John Gordon, *History of New England*, Little Brown, Boston, Mass., 1860.

Penny, Norman, *The First Publisher of the Truth, Early Records of the Introduction of Quakerism*, Headley Bros, London, 1967.

Peterson, Rev., Ed, *Rhode Island and Newport*, John S. Taylor, New York, 1850.

Pew, General William A., *The Worshipful Simon Bradstreet*, New Comb & Gauss, Salem, Mass., 1928.

Piercy, Josephine K., *Anne Bradstreet*, Twayne Pub., 31 Union Square, New

York, N.Y.

Plumley, Ruth, *Lays of Quakerdom*, Riddle Press, Philadelphia, Penn..

Preston, Howard Willard, *Rhode Island and the Sea*, State Bureau of Life, Providence, R.I., 1632.

Purver, Margery, *The Royal Society, Concept and Creation*, MIT Press, Cambridge, Mass., 1967.

Records of the Colony of Rhode Island and Providence Plantations in New England. 1636-1663. Printed by order of the Legislature, transcribed and edited by John Russell Bartlett, A. Crawford Greene and Brother, State Printers, Providence, R.I., 1857,

Richman, Irving Berdine, *Rhode Island, Its Making and Meaning*, Knickerbocker Press, New York, London, 1902.

Rickman, John MD, *Need for a Belief in God*, Basic Books, New York, N.Y., 1957.

Rogers, Horatio, *Mary Dyer of Rhode Island, The Quaker Martyr That Was Hanged on Boston Commons*, Preston Round, Providence, R.I., 1896.

Ross, Isabel, *Margaret Askew Fell, Mother of Quakerism*, Longmans Green, London, 1947.

Rogers, Horatio, *Mary Dyer of Rhode Island*, Norwood Press, Norwood, Mass, 1896.

Ross, Isabel, *Mary Askew Fell, Mother of Quakerism*, Longman Green, London, 1949.

Rossiter, Clinton, *The First American Revolution*, Harcourt Brace, New York, N.Y., 1953.

Rugg, Winifred King, Unafraid *A Life of Anne Hutchinson*, Houghton Mifflin, 1930.

Rutman, Darret B., *Winthrop's Boston*, University of North Carolina, 1965.

Ryder, Sidney, S., *The Lands of Rhode Island as the Great Sachems Knew Them*, Providence, R.I., 1964.

Selleck, George, *Quakers in Boston 1656-1964*, Friends Meeting, Cambridge, 1976.

Sewell, Samuel, *Diary* (edited by Mark Van Dorean), Mary Masino, New York, N.Y., 1927.

Sewell, William, *A History of the Quakers*, London, 1718.

Sheffield, William P., *Rhode Island, Privateerism of Newport*, Rhode Island Historical Society, Newport, R.I., 1883.

_____, *Random Notes on the Government of Rhode Island*, Newport, R.I., 1897.

Spence Manuscripts, Friends Library, London.

St. George, Robert Blair, *Material Life in America*, 1600-1860, Northeastern University Press, Boston, 1988.

Stephenson, Marmaduke, *A Call from Death to Life*, Augerville Society, Edinburgh, 1886.

Straus, Oscar Solomon, Roger Williams, *Pioneer of Religious Liberty*, Century, N.Y., 1895.

Swarthmore Manuscripts, Friends Library, London.

Taylor, John, *An Account of Some of the Labours, Exercises, and Perils by Sea and Land*, J. Bolwer in Whithare Court in Gracious Street MDCCS, London.

Terry, R., *The Commission of Governor Coddington and the Early Charters of Rhode Island*, Newport Historical Society, Bulletin 44123.

_____, Influences Leading to First Settlement of Newport, Newport Historical Society.

Vipont, Efrida, *George Fox and the Valiant 60*, Hamish Hamilton, London, 1975.

Weeden, William Babcock, *Early Rhode Island*, Grafton Press, New York, N.Y.

_____, *Economic and Social History of New England*, Houghton Mifflin, 1890.

White, Ethel, *Bear His Mild Yoke*, Abingdon Press, Nashville, N.Y., 1966.

Whitehall, Walter M. Boston, *A Topographical History*, Cambridge, Belknap Press, Harvard University Press, 1959.

Whittier, John Greenleaf, *Margaret Smith's Journal*, Houghton Mifflin, 1866.

Williams, *Emily Coddington, William Coddington*, privately printed, Newport, R.I., 1941.

Williams, Roger, *The Complete Writings of Roger Williams*, Russell & Russell, New York, 1963.

Vol. 1: *Key into the Language of America, 1642*

Vol. 2: *John Cotter's Answer to Roger Williams*

Vol. 3: *The Bloody Tenent of Persecution, 1643*

Vol. 4: *The Bloody Tenent Yet More Bloody*

Vol. 5: *George Fox Digg'd Out of his Burrows, 1672*

Vol. 6: *Letters of Roger Williams*

Vol. 7: *Experiment in Spiritual Life and Health, 1652*

Williams, Selma, *Divine Rebel, Life of Anne Marbury Hutchinson*, Holt Rinehart, N.Y., 1981.

Williamson, Hugh Ross, *The Day They Killed the King*, MacMillan, New

York, N.Y., 1957.

Willison, George, *Saints and Strangers*, Reynal & Hitchcock, New York, N.Y., 1945.

Wilson, Lela Morse, *Ten Generations from William and Mary Dyer*, Putnam Conn., 1949.

Winslow, Edward, *Good News from New England*, Dawson, London, 1624.

Winslow, Ola Elisabeth, *Master Roger Williams*, MacMillan, New York, N.Y., 1957.

Winsor, Justin, *Memorial History of Boston* (1630-80), Ticknor & Company, Boston, 1850.

Winsor, John, *History of New England*, Winthrop Papers, Massachusetts Historical Society, 1944.

Winthrop, John, Journal,The History of New England, 1630-1649, and Short Story of the Rise, Reign and Ruin of Antinomians, Vol. 1 & 2, Phelps & Farnham, 5 Court Street, Boston, 1825.

_____, *Journal and Short Story*, edited by James Kendall Hosmer, Charles Scribner's Sons, New York, 1908.

Witele, John Charles, *Lives and Identities of the Indians of Shelter Island, 1652-1830*, Long Island Historical Journal, Department of History, State University of New York, Stony Brook.

Wood, William, *New England Prospects*, London, 1634.

Index